Contents

1 Creating Documents

1

2 Formatting Documents

28

3 Advanced Editing and Multiple Files

Introducing

Microsoft Word 6.0

FOR

WINDOWS

KEIKO PITTER

McGRAW-HILL
New York St. Louis San Francisco Auckland Bogotá Caracas
Lisbon London Madrid Mexico Milan Montreal New Delhi
Paris San Juan Singapore Sydney Tokyo Toronto

McGRAW-HILL
San Francisco, CA 94133

Introducing Microsoft Word 6.0 for Windows

1 2 3 4 5 6 7 8 9 0   SEM SEM   9 0 9 8 7 6 5 4

ISBN 0-07-051767-3

Sponsoring editor: Roger Howell
Editorial assistant: Rhonda Sands
Technical reviewer: Sarah Baker
Production supervisor: Leslie Austin
Project manager: Maria Takacs, Graphics West
Copyeditor: Ryan Stuart
Interior designer: Gary Palmatier
Cover designer: Christy Butterfield
Compositor: Graphics West
Printer and binder: Semline, Inc.

Library of Congress Card Catalog No. 94-77137

Graphics, Columns, Templates, and Tables

84

Introduction

A word processing program is a computer program that helps you create, change, and print text. Word processing simplifies the mechanics of preparing documents and helps you to focus on the process of writing.

Introducing Microsoft Word 6.0 for Windows acquaints you with the essential information necessary to create simple to sophisticated documents. Working within the graphical environment of Windows, Word commands and features are presented to increase user knowledge and expertise. This manual is designed to get the user comfortable with the essentials of Microsoft Word 6.0 for Windows and feel confident in exploring the program's capabilities. Not all features of Word 6.0 are covered, and when there is more than one way to accomplish a task, just one method is discussed. The user needs to explore others on his or her own.

Using this Module

Each lesson in this book begins with goals that are listed under the heading *OBJECTIVES*. Key terms are introduced in ***bold italic*** type; text to be typed by the user is shown in **bold**. Also, keep in mind the following:

■   This symbol is used to indicate the user's action.

▶   *This symbol is used to indicate the software's response.*

Alternative: **Presents mouse or keystroke alternatives to keyboard commands.**

N O T E :   This format is for important user notes and tips.

P R A C T I C E   T I M E

These brief drills allow the user to practice features previously discussed.

Finally, a series of projects, a command summary, and a glossary of key terms are found at the end of the book.

BEFORE YOU START

To use this book, you need at least an 80286 or higher with at least 4 MG of memory (RAM). If you are installing the program, you need at least 6 MB of space available on your hard disk (the complete installation requires 24 MB of disk space). The computer should also have a floppy disk drive (1.2 MB or greater capacity), a mouse or other pointing device, Windows 3.1 or later, and Microsoft Word for Windows 6.0. The user needs to have a blank, formatted floppy disk. If your configuration deviates from this, consult your instructor. This book assumes that you are familiar with both the basic operation of a computer system and of Microsoft Windows, and with how to use a mouse.

To study this book, you should go through Lessons 1, 2, and the first half of 3. These lessons acquaint you with the basics of word processing. The optional second half of Lesson 3 introduces the merge feature, and Lesson 4 introduces the use of templates, graphics, columns, and tables.

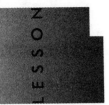

LESSON

Creating Documents

OBJECTIVES

Upon completion of the material presented in this lesson, you should understand the following aspects of Microsoft Word:

- ☐ **Starting Microsoft Word**
- ☐ **Comprehending word processing terminology**
- ☐ **Giving Microsoft Word commands**
- ☐ **Entering text**
- ☐ **Saving a file to a disk**
- ☐ **Moving through the document**
- ☐ **Selecting text**
- ☐ **Deleting selected text**
- ☐ **Replacing selected text**
- ☐ **Moving and Copying selected text**
- ☐ **Inserting text in an existing document**
- ☐ **Checking the spelling**
- ☐ **Using the Thesaurus**
- ☐ **Previewing and printing the document**

STARTING OFF

Before starting Microsoft Word, you must start the Microsoft Windows program.

■ Start the Windows program. Make sure that the Program Manager is the only window displayed onscreen.

▶ *The installation procedure for Microsoft Word created a program group icon for Word for Windows in the Program Manager window. See Figure 1-1.*

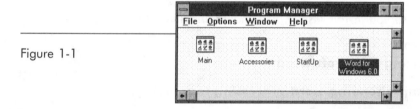

Figure 1-1

NOTE: It is possible that Microsoft Word was installed in the Microsoft Office group window. If so, substitute the appropriate group name in the instruction.

■ Maximize the Program Manager window.

■ Open the Microsoft Word window by double-clicking on the Word for Windows group icon.

▶ *The Word for Windows window, similar to the one in Figure 1-2, is displayed.*

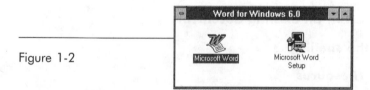

Figure 1-2

The Microsoft Word program group window contains the Word program icon. To start Microsoft Word, double-click on it.

■ Launch the Microsoft Word program by double-clicking on the Microsoft Word program icon.

▶ *If your program is so set up, the Tip of the Day is displayed. Close the dialog box by clicking on OK or pressing* Enter. *The Microsoft Word application window is displayed as shown in Figure 1-3.*

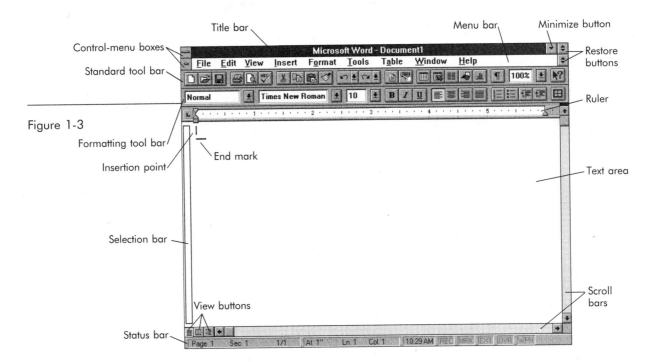

Figure 1-3

The Microsoft Word application window has all the basic components of a Windows window—a title bar, a menu bar, a control-menu box, minimize, maximize, and restore buttons, and scroll bars. There are additional elements, such as the **toolbars** and **ruler** below the menu bar, and the **status bar** at the bottom. These will be explained later.

You might notice that there are two restore buttons and two control-menu boxes. This is because, onscreen right now are two windows displayed: the Microsoft Word application window and a new document window. The new document window is contained within the workspace, or the area between the menu bar and the status bar, of the Microsoft Word application window, and the new document window is already maximized.

■ Restore the document window by clicking on the lower restore button.

▶ *The document window is restored, as shown in Figure 1-4.*

Now you can see the document window more distinctly. The workspace can contain up to nine documents if your computer has enough available memory. You might notice that the title bar of the Microsoft Word application window displays Microsoft Word, and that of the document window contains the name Document1.

Figure 1-4

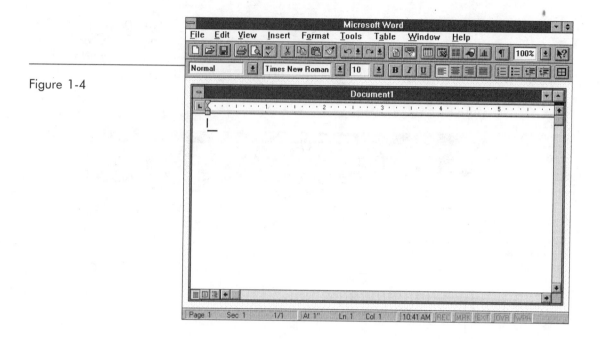

■   Maximize the document window.

▶   *Notice that the title bar is changed to Microsoft Word -
    Document1 and that the new document window filled out
    the workspace.*

The ***menu bar***, located below the title bar, contains nine menu options. Microsoft Word commands are accessed either by clicking on the
desired menu option or by pressing the ⌊Alt⌋ key and the key of the underlined letter in the menu option you want. When you select a menu option, a
menu containing the commands, called ***drop-down menu***, appears below
the option.

■   Select the Edit option on the menu bar by clicking on it or by
    holding down the ⌊Alt⌋ key and pressing ⌊E⌋.

▶   *A drop-down menu appears, as shown in Figure 1-5.*

You can make a selection from the drop-down menu by clicking on a
command or pressing the key of the underlined letter in the command.
Commands that are dimmed are not available to you at this point. (They
require that you've performed some other action.)

Commands followed by an ellipsis (...) will display a ***dialog box*** in
which you are required to enter additional information such as the name to
call a document. Dialog boxes will be explained as you encounter them in
the lesson.

You will notice that some commands are ***toggles***, which means the
command turns a feature on or off each time you enter it. When a toggle
feature is on, a check mark appears before the command option in the
menu, and the check mark disappears when the feature is turned off. In

Figure 1-5

Edit	
Can't Undo	Ctrl+Z
Repeat Typing	Ctrl+Y
Cut	Ctrl+X
Copy	Ctrl+C
Paste	Ctrl+V
Paste Special...	
Clear	Delete
Select A**ll**	Ctrl+A
Find...	Ctrl+F
R**e**place...	Ctrl+H
Go To...	Ctrl+G
AutoText...	
Bookmark...	
Links...	
Object	

other cases, you need to make a selection from a number of options. The selected option will have a bullet (•) displayed before it.

Many commands offer you alternative keystrokes. These appear next to the corresponding command in the drop-down menu. That is, rather than making a selection from the menu bar and from the drop-down menu, commands can be entered by clicking on a tool button or pressing a key in combination with (Ctrl), (Shift), and (Alt) keys. When you see (Shift)+(F12), for example, you are to hold down the key marked (Shift) and press the (F12) function key; when you see (Ctrl)+(X), you hold down the key marked (Ctrl) and press (X). These available tool buttons and alternative keys will be given.

To close a menu without choosing a command, click outside the menu or press the (Esc) key.

■   Close the drop-down menu.

Below the menu bar are two Tool bars: the standard toolbar and the formatting toolbar. They contain buttons that give you quick access to frequently-used commands.

■   Move the mouse pointer on top of the first tool button and let it sit for a moment.

▶   *A description of the button pops up, as shown in Figure 1-6.*

The ruler displays and allows you to change the margins, tabs, and indentation setting.

N O T E :   The toolbars and ruler can be hidden from display.

The area below the ruler is the ***text area***. This is the area in which you can enter new text or graphics, review what you have already entered, or change what is there. Of course, as you have not entered anything yet, it is blank. The blinking vertical bar is the ***insertion point***, and the underscore is the ***end mark***. The insertion point shows the position in the workspace where entries are made, and the end mark identifies the end of your document.

Along the left side of the text area is an unmarked area called the ***selection bar***. It helps you select text with the mouse. When the mouse

Figure 1-6

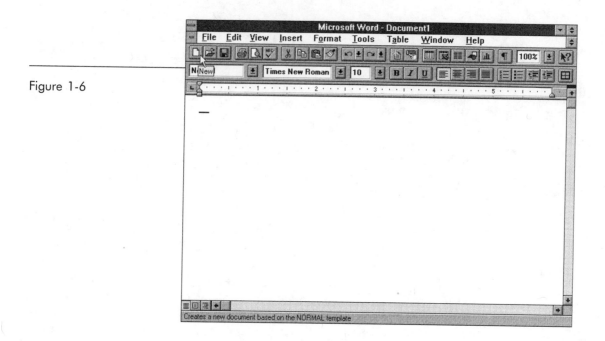

pointer is in the text area, it turns into an I-beam. However, when it is in the selection bar, it turns into a right pointing arrow ∿.

To the left of the horizontal scroll bar at the bottom are three buttons: Normal View, Page Layout View, and Outline View. These are used to change the way the document is displayed.

At the bottom of the screen is the status bar. It displays the following information about the page that contains the insertion point: the page number; the section number; the total number of pages from the beginning of the document followed by the total number of pages in the entire document; the position of the insertion point measured from the top edge of the page; the line number; and the column number calculated by counting the number of characters between the insertion point and the left margin. It also shows the status of several key on your computer, such as Caps Lock and Num Lock, and of various Word features.

ENTERING TEXT

To enter text, use your keyboard similar to the way you would use a typewriter. As you enter a character, it appears at the insertion point, and the insertion point moves to the right one position. Unlike the keyboard on a typewriter, however, this keyboard does not require entry of a carriage return as you fill a line onscreen. Just keep on typing, because when the cursor gets beyond the right margin, it will reappear at the left margin setting, one line down. When you come to the end of a paragraph, the Enter key must be pressed. The Enter key breaks the line and moves the insertion point to the left margin, one line down. You have to press the [Enter] key once at the end of a paragraph. Press [Enter] twice if you want to insert a blank line between paragraphs in the text.

If your text fills up the screen, the text will *scroll* up—that is, a new line will appear at the bottom of the screen, and the uppermost line will disappear from view.

CORRECTING ERRORS

If you make a mistake when you are typing text, you may delete unwanted characters by pressing the [Bksp] key. [Bksp] deletes the key to the left of the insertion point. You can then retype the text.

UPPERCASE LETTERS

To enter uppercase letters, hold [Shift] down while you press the character. If you want to type several characters in uppercase, as when you enter a title, press [Caps Lock]. To get back into lowercase, press [Caps Lock] again. When you enter certain characters, you have to hold [Shift] down regardless of whether [Caps Lock] has been pressed.

P R A C T I C E   T I M E   1 - 1

Enter the following text:

Records of transactions, contracts, and inventories form the basis that allows business to be conducted in an orderly manner. Scribes have been used through the ages to produce copies of business contracts. Inventions that have lowered the cost or increased the speed for an individual to write a document have resulted in increased business productivity. These inventions include paper, pens, and typewriter. The personal computer did not become a success until it became useful for business. Today, word processing is the most common business use of personal computers.

As you typed in this paragraph, you might have noticed the phenomenon called ***wordwrap***. As the text gets to the right margin, a word that is too long to fit on the line is moved down to the next line. Words are not split between lines. This feature is included to make reading and text creation easier.

SAVING YOUR WORK

The text that you have just entered is stored in the main memory of the computer. If you turn off the computer or if there is a power failure, you will lose that text. That is why it is important that you save the file on a disk, not only when you quit Microsoft Word, but frequently during your Microsoft Word session. Once a file is on a disk, it is permanently stored. Should there be a power failure, you can retrieve the most recent version of the file from the disk and continue with your work.

NOTE: This manual assumes that your data disk is in drive A. If you are using a drive other than A, substitute the appropriate drive in the instructions.

■   Make sure a formatted disk is in drive A.

When you save a file, you have two choices: you can use the Save command or the Save As command. If you use the Save command, the file is saved using the filename that appears in the title bar. If there already is a file by that name on the disk, the new file will replace the existing file. If you use the Save As command, you must type a new name for your file.

The first time you save a document, you are forced to use the Save As command no matter which save option you selected. This is to be sure that you give a meaningful name to the document rather than the default name assigned by Microsoft Word.

As mentioned earlier, when you start a new file, Microsoft Word automatically gives it a default name, such as Document1. When you save the file for the first time, you use the Save As command and give it a valid and more meaningful name. A valid name for the document, known as the filename, is one to eight characters in number, followed by an optional extension. The extension is a period (.) and one to three additional characters. If you do not supply an extension, Microsoft Word automatically assigns the extension .DOC. You can use any character except spaces and the following characters: * ? , ; [ ] + = \ / : ¦ < >. You cannot use a period except to separate the filename from the extension. Right now, use the name MYFILE to save it to the disk in drive A.

■   Select the <u>F</u>ile menu in the menu bar by clicking on it or by pressing Alt + F, then select Save <u>A</u>s by clicking on it or by pressing **A**.

Alternative: Click on the Save tool button 🔲.

▶ *The Save As dialog box is displayed as shown in Figure 1-7.*

Figure 1-7

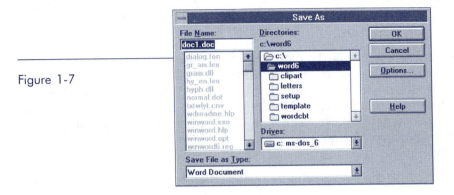

NOTE: Using the Save tool button has the same effect as using the Save command. The file is saved using the current filename.

The insertion point is blinking in the File Name text box. Type the filename, but do not press Enter.

■ Type **MYFILE**, but do not press Enter.

You need to specify the location of the data disk.

■ Click on the down arrow key at the right end of the Drives list box.

▶ *All available drives are displayed.*

■ Click on a: for drive A.

▶ *The Directories list box displays all directories currently on drive A. If you need to specify the directory, do so by clicking on the directory name.*

■ Complete the command by either clicking on the OK button or pressing Enter.

▶ *The file is saved to the disk in drive A.*

MOVING WITHIN THE DOCUMENT

Suppose, as you read what you typed earlier, you find a mistake or you decide to change the text. If the change you want to make is near the beginning of the text, and if you use the Bksp key to erase all unwanted characters starting at the insertion point, you will have to retype almost the whole text. This is no improvement over using a typewriter. A word processor has a better way. To make corrections like this, you need to learn how to move within the document. That is, you need to learn how to move the insertion point. Text is entered, deleted, or edited at the insertion point.

Using the Mouse

The insertion point may be moved by positioning the I-beam in the desired place and clicking the left mouse button once. If the desired text position has scrolled off the screen, bring it back to the display by clicking on the scroll arrows at either end of the vertical scroll bar at the window's right. When you scroll the text display, however, the insertion point stays in its original position and does not move. Hence, you need to specify the new insertion point.

■   Use the mouse to move the insertion point.

Using the Keyboard

To move the insertion point, use the four arrow keys located on the numeric keypad to the right of the main keyboard (or the arrow keys located between the main keyboard and the numeric keyboard on extended keyboards). The insertion point will move in the direction of the arrow, one position at a time.

N O T E :   If you are using the numeric keypad, make sure that Num Lock is turned off.

■   Press ↑.

▶   *The insertion point moves up one line.*

■   Press →.

▶   *The insertion point moves to the right one position.*

If you have a long text, you cannot see all of it onscreen at any one time. As you press ↑ or ↓ repeatedly, the insertion point will keep moving up or down, forcing the screen to scroll. If you keep pressing ↑, the text will scroll down (that is, new lines will appear at the top); if you keep pressing ↓, the text will scroll up (new lines will appear at the bottom).

N O T E :   You will quickly learn that the movement of text onscreen is in the direction opposite to the label on the key. The ↑ key lets you view text that was above the screen, and ↓ brings into view text that was below the screen.

It is also possible to move the insertion point a little faster. All you have to do is hold the key down, and the key will keep repeating. If you hold down ↓, the insertion point will zoom down the page. You can return it to the top of the page by using ↑. You will notice, however, that you cannot move the insertion point past the beginning or the end of the text.

You can move the insertion point to the left or right, one word at a time, by holding down the Ctrl key and pressing ← and →, respectively.

NOTE: On some computers, when giving a combination command with arrow keys, Num Lock must be turned off regardless of which set of arrow keys is used. On other computers, the combination only works with the arrow keys on the numeric keypad.

You can move the insertion point to the beginning of the document by pressing Ctrl+Home. That is, hold Ctrl down while you press Home. You can move it to the end of the document by pressing Ctrl+End. Table 1-1 lists various keystrokes for moving the insertion point. (The text you see onscreen right now is not long enough for you to try all of these keys. Just remember them for the future.)

Table 1-1

Key	Action
→	Moves one character to the right
←	Moves one character to the left
↑	Moves one line up
↓	Moves one line down
Ctrl+Home	Moves to the beginning of a document
Ctrl+End	Moves to the end of a document
Ctrl+→	Moves one word to the right
Ctrl+←	Moves one word to the left
Home	Moves to the beginning of a line
End	Moves to the end of a line
Ctrl+↑	Moves up one paragraph
Pg Dn	Moves down one window
Pg Up	Moves up one window

PRACTICE TIME 1-2

1. Move the insertion point to the end, and then to the beginning, of the document.

2. Place the insertion point somewhere in the middle of the document.

3. Try using both keyboard and mouse to move the insertion point.

DELETING TEXT

As you recall, if you make a mistake in typing text, you can correct it immediately by pressing the [Bksp] to remove the unwanted characters, then typing the correct text.

You may delete unwanted characters *anywhere* in the text by adding one step. First, position the insertion point next to the character you wish to delete. Second, press the [Bksp] key to erase the character to the left and the [Del] key to erase the character to the right of the insertion point. Finally, type the correct text.

You can delete text from the keyboard in other ways, too. You can remove the word before the insertion point by entering [Ctrl]+[Bksp], that is, holding down the [Ctrl] key and pressing [Bksp]. You can remove the word after the insertion point by entering [Ctrl]+[Del], that is, holding down the [Ctrl] key and pressing the [Del] key. You can also delete a selected section of text.

SELECTING TEXT

You will now select the sentence beginning "Scribes have ...."

■ Position the insertion point to the left of the capital S of "Scribes have...," then drag the mouse to highlight the entire sentence. To do this, hold down the left mouse button, move the mouse until the sentence is highlighted, then release the button.

Alternative: **Position the insertion point anywhere in the sentence, then press** [Ctrl]**+click (hold down the** [Ctrl] **key and click the left mouse button).**

▶ *The sentence is selected, as shown in Figure 1-8.*

Figure 1-8

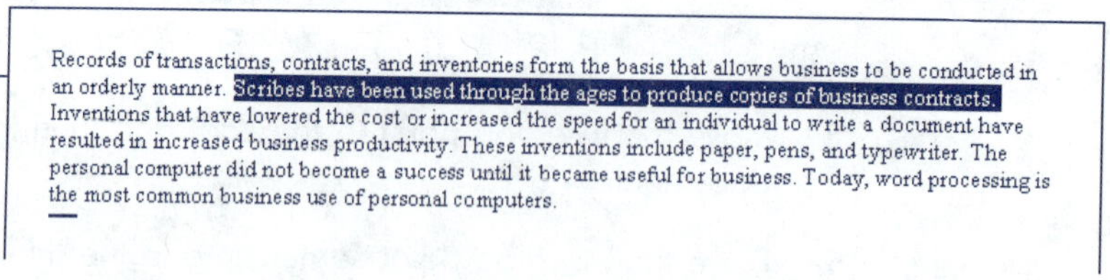

Records of transactions, contracts, and inventories form the basis that allows business to be conducted in an orderly manner. Scribes have been used through the ages to produce copies of business contracts. Inventions that have lowered the cost or increased the speed for an individual to write a document have resulted in increased business productivity. These inventions include paper, pens, and typewriter. The personal computer did not become a success until it became useful for business. Today, word processing is the most common business use of personal computers.

N O T E :   If you selected the wrong text, click elsewhere onscreen or press an arrow key to deselect.

Another way to select text is by using the selection bar, which is an unmarked area along the left side of the text area. Once in the selection bar, the pointer shape changes to a right-pointing arrow. Using the selection bar and mouse, you can select a line, paragraph, or entire document with one or two mouse clicks.

Table 1-2 shows ways of selecting text using the selection bar and mouse, as well as keyboard.

Table 1-2

Using Mouse	**Select**	**Using Keyboard**	**Select**
Double-click	Word	Shift + →	One character to the right
Ctrl + click anywhere in sentence	Sentence	Shift + ←	One character to the left
		Shift + ↑	One line up
		Shift + ↓	One line down
Place pointer in the selection bar, point to line, and click	Line	Shift + End	To the end of a line
		Shift + Home	To the start of a line
		Shift + Pg Up	One screen up
		Shift + Pg Dn	One screen down
Place pointer in the selection bar, point to paragraph, and double-click	Paragraph	Shift + Ctrl + →	To the end of a word
		Shift + Ctrl + ←	To the start of a word
		Shift + Ctrl + ↑	To the start of a paragraph
		Shift + Ctrl + ↓	To the end of a paragraph
Ctrl + click anywhere in the selection bar	Document	Shift + Ctrl + Home	To the start of a document
		Shift + Ctrl + End	To the end of a document
		Ctrl + A	An entire document

DELETING SELECTED TEXT

Once text is selected, it can be deleted.

■   Press either Bksp or Del to delete the selected text. Do not move the insertion point.

RESTORING DELETED TEXT

If you realize you didn't mean to remove the text after you've deleted it, you can restore it immediately by using the Undo command.

■   Click on Edit, then on Undo Typing.

Alternative: **Press Ctrl + Z or click on the Undo Tool button** 🔄.

▶   *The text is restored.*

P R A C T I C E   T I M E   1 - 3

Delete the second sentence again.

REPLACING TEXT

You can easily replace a word or phrase with different text.

- ■ Select the text "personal computer" in the next-to-last sentence.
- ■ Type **microcomputer**.

  ▶ *The highlighted text is deleted and replaced by what you typed.*

P R A C T I C E   T I M E   1 - 4

Change "microcomputer" back to "personal computer."

MOVING TEXT

You can also move the selected text from one location to another. This is done using the Cut and Paste commands. The Cut command removes the selected text from a document and places the selection on the Windows *clipboard*, which is temporary storage for information you want to transfer. You can then paste the information where you specify.

Right now, you will move the last sentence.

- ■ Select the last sentence, "Today, word processing is the most common business use of personal computers," as shown in Figure 1-9.

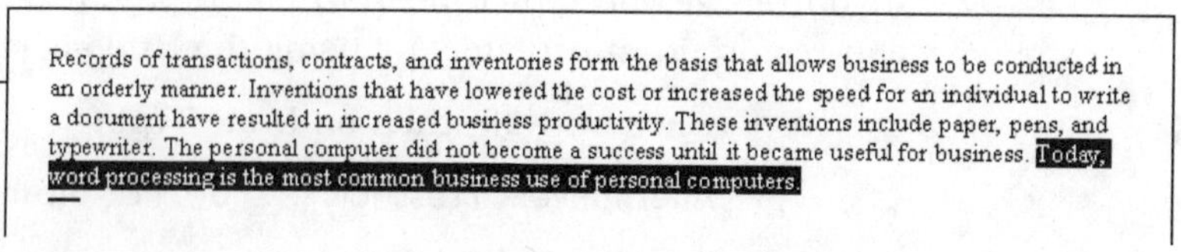

Figure 1-9

Records of transactions, contracts, and inventories form the basis that allows business to be conducted in an orderly manner. Inventions that have lowered the cost or increased the speed for an individual to write a document have resulted in increased business productivity. These inventions include paper, pens, and typewriter. The personal computer did not become a success until it became useful for business. Today, word processing is the most common business use of personal computers.

■ From the <u>E</u>dit menu, select Cu<u>t</u>.

Alternative: Press Ctrl+X or click the Cut tool button 🔧.

▶ *The selected text disappears; it has been placed on the clipboard.*

■ Move the insertion point to the space just before the fourth sentence—that is, after the word "typewriter."

■ From the <u>E</u>dit menu, select <u>P</u>aste.

Alternative: Enter Ctrl+V or click the Paste tool button 📋.

▶ *The text is placed at the insertion point position as shown in Figure 1-10. You may have to insert or delete spaces to make sentence display correctly.*

Figure 1-10

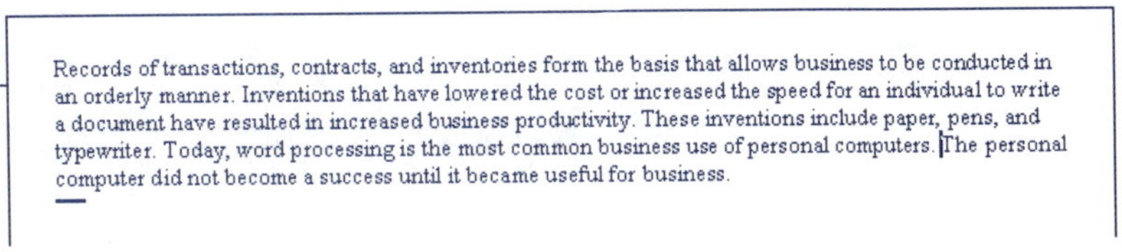

> Records of transactions, contracts, and inventories form the basis that allows business to be conducted in an orderly manner. Inventions that have lowered the cost or increased the speed for an individual to write a document have resulted in increased business productivity. These inventions include paper, pens, and typewriter. Today, word processing is the most common business use of personal computers. The personal computer did not become a success until it became useful for business.

N O T E :   To easily access the Copy and Paste commands, you can place the mouse pointer over the highlighted text and press the *right* mouse button. A Shortcut menu appears, as shown in Figure 1-11. The Shortcut menu contains commands related to the item you're working with.

Figure 1-11

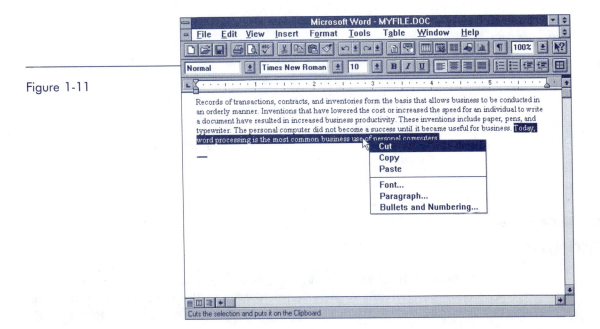

DRAG AND DROP

You will now move the sentence you just moved back to its original position, but using a different method. With ***drag and drop***, you can select the text and drag it to where you want it.

■ Select the same sentence.

■ Position the mouse pointer anywhere on the highlighted text and press the *left* mouse button.

▶ *The mouse pointer changes to indicate that you can drag the text, as shown in Figure 1-12.*

Figure 1-12

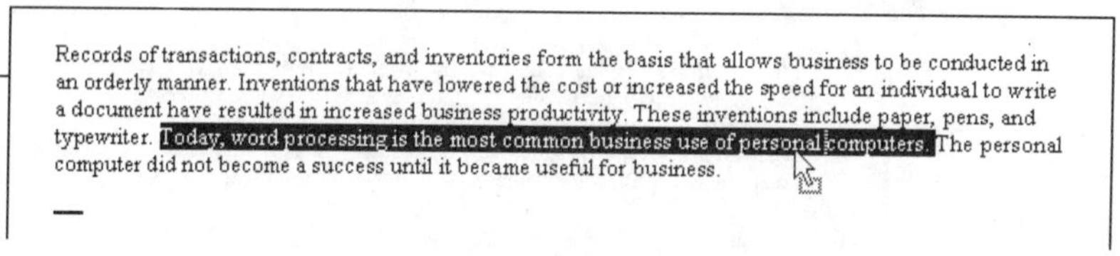

> Records of transactions, contracts, and inventories form the basis that allows business to be conducted in an orderly manner. Inventions that have lowered the cost or increased the speed for an individual to write a document have resulted in increased business productivity. These inventions include paper, pens, and typewriter. Today, word processing is the most common business use of personal computers. The personal computer did not become a success until it became useful for business.

■ Drag the mouse pointer, that is, hold down the left mouse button and move the insertion point to the desired position, which in this case is after the last sentence.

■ Release the mouse button.

▶ *The sentence is moved.*

COPYING TEXT

It is also possible to copy selected text. Copying text is different from moving text, in that selected text is not deleted from the original position. To do this, select Copy from the Edit menu, instead of Cut. You can also use the Copy button 🗐. If you want to use the drag and drop feature, hold down Ctrl while you drag the mouse.

INSERTING TEXT

If you need to insert a word in the middle of a sentence, or a sentence in the middle of a paragraph, position the insertion point where you want to begin inserting the text, then look at the status bar. If you see the letters OVR, press the [Ins] key. When you press [Ins], the letters OVR disappear. Then you can start typing whatever you want to insert at the insertion point position.

When OVR is not on, any text to the right of the insertion point is pushed across the line to make room for your insertion. When OVR is on, however, the character you type replaces the character the insertion point is on. [Ins] is a toggle command. The feature is turned on and off each time you press the [Ins] key.

■ Place the insertion point just before the word "Inventions" in the second sentence.

■ Insert the following text just as it appears, *with* the spelling errors:

The earliest writing, cuneiform inscriptoins on on clay tablets, often kept business recrds.

CHECKING SPELLING

Microsoft Word can check your document for misspelled words, two occurrences of a word in a row, and certain types of capitalization errors. The feature helps you proof the document onscreen by comparing each word in the document with a list of correctly spelled words, known as a **dictionary**. When you issue the Spelling command, the program scans the document, flags those words that are not in the dictionary, and for each of these words, suggests words from the dictionary that you might have meant to type.

N O T E :   If a word is not in the MS Word dictionary, such as a proper name or a term that is special to a particular industry, Word will flag it as misspelled. You have the option of adding it to a custom dictionary. Once added, the next occurrence of the same word is not flagged.

The program checks the entire document, starting at the insertion point. If you start at the middle, when Word gets to the end of the document, it will ask you if you want to continue checking at the beginning of the document. If you do not want to check all of your document, select that part of document you want to check, then give the Spelling command.

You entered some words with spelling errors in the current document. You will now correct them.

■ Position the insertion point at the beginning of the document.

■ From the Tools menu, select Spelling.

Alternative: Press the [F7] function key or click the Spelling tool button.

> ▶ *The Spelling dialog box is displayed as shown in Figure 1-13.*

Figure 1-13

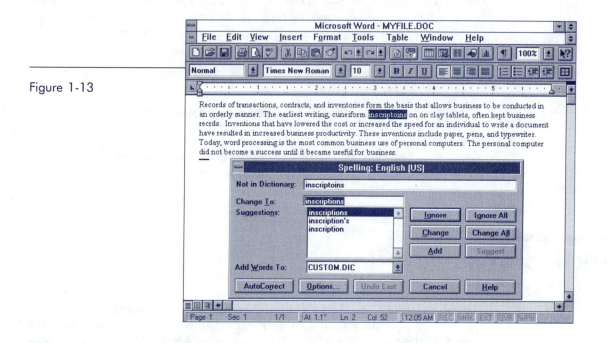

The word "inscriptoins" is highlighted in the document and appears in the Not in Dictionary text box. In the Suggestions list box, the word "inscriptions" is listed and highlighted. As the highlighted word, it also appears in the Changes To text box. Since the highlighted word is correctly spelled, tell Word to replace it in the document.

■ Select the <u>C</u>hange button by clicking on it or by pressing [Alt]+[C].

> ▶ *The correctly-spelled word is inserted. Now the word "on" is highlighted in the document.*

N O T E :   If you were to click on Change All instead, all instances of the same word subsequently found in your document are corrected.

Word now tells you that the word "on" is a repeated word. That is, it appears twice in a row. You want to delete the second occurrence.

■ Select the <u>D</u>elete button by clicking on it or pressing [Alt]+[D].

> ▶ *The second "on" is deleted. Now the word "recrds" is highlighted.*

PRACTICE TIME 1-5

Replace the word "recrds" with the correctly-spelled word. When Word is finished checking spelling, a dialog box appears to notify you. Respond accordingly.

If a word is flagged but is spelled correctly or if a suggested spelling is not given, that word is not currently contained in the dictionary. You can do one of four things: (1) you can add it to a Custom Dictionary by selecting the Add button; (2) you can tell Word to ignore the occurrence of this word this one time by clicking the Ignore button; (3) you can tell Word to ignore the occurrence of this word for the rest of the document by clicking the Ignore All button; or (4) you can edit the word manually. To edit the word manually, place the insertion point in the Change To text box by using the mouse, edit the word, then click the Change option.

After you finish entering text, you should always run it through the spelling checker. It does not catch all your mistakes. For example, if you used "their" for "there," because the word is correctly spelled, the mistake is not caught, but it is still a good aid in creating an accurate document.

THESAURUS

One more available feature should be mentioned: the Thesaurus. Many times, when you are writing a document, you need help finding a word to express your meaning more clearly. The Thesaurus displays synonyms and other words that point to the same idea.

Assume that in the onscreen text, you decide that the word "contracts" in the first sentence is not quite what you wanted to say.

■　Place the insertion point anywhere on the word "contracts".

■　From the Tools menu, select Thesaurus.

　　Alternative:　**Press** (Shift)+(F7).

▶　*The Thesaurus dialog box is displayed, as shown in Figure 1-14.*

In the dialog box, Word is now saying that the word "contracts" does not appear in the Thesaurus. However, it lists the singular form "contract" as a related word. You can look up a related word in the Thesaurus.

■　Select the Look Up button.

▶　*Both list boxes display various options for "contract."*

Figure 1-14

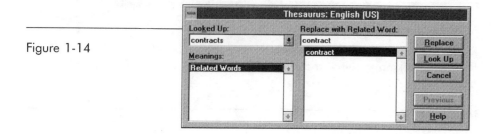

The Meanings list box displays different meanings of the word. These include the use of the word as a noun or verb. The list also includes an antonym, or a word with the opposite meaning, and other related words. The Synonyms list box displays words with the selected meaning. The highlighted word in the Synonyms list box also appears in the Replace With text box.

As you select different meanings in the Meanings list box, the content of the Synonyms list box changes to display words with the selected meaning. If you see the word you are looking for in the Synonyms list, select it and click the Replace button. For example, if the word you want to use is "agreement," select it by clicking on it, then click the Replace button. The word "contracts" in the text will be replaced by "agreement." If you did not find the word you are looking for in this list, you can continue the search by doing a Look Up on any of the words listed.

■   Make sure that "agreement" is selected in the Replace with Synonym list box and select the Replace button.

▶   *The word is replaced.*

Because Microsoft Word inserted the singular word "agreement," you will have to enter an "s" at the end to make it plural, in keeping with the rest of the sentence.

■   Insert **s** after "agreement" to make it plural.

SAVING A FILE THE SECOND TIME

Now that you've made several changes to your file, you should save it again. This time, you will save using the same filename.

■   Make sure that the data disk is in drive A.

■   From the File menu, select Save.

Alternative: Press Ctrl+S or click the Save tool button.

▶   *The current document replaces the one on the data disk.*

PREVIEWING TEXT

Before printing the text on a sheet of paper, you can view it onscreen. This is called previewing text.

■   From the <u>F</u>ile menu, select Print Pre<u>v</u>iew.

Alternative: **Click on the Print Preview button** 🔍.

▶   *A screen similar to Figure 1-15 is displayed. Notice that the mouse pointer turns into a magnifying glass when it's at the top of the document.*

Figure 1-15

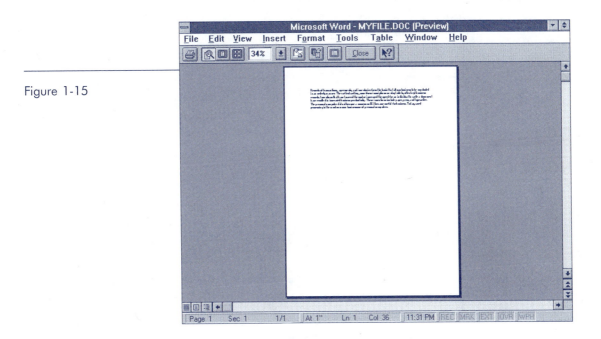

The screen displays the way your page will look when it is printed. However, the type is too small to read. You can enlarge the display.

■   With the mouse pointer anywhere on the text in the document, click the left mouse button.

▶   *The display is enlarged as shown in Figure 1-16.*

■   Click on the document again.

▶   *The display returns to normal view.*

If you are satisfied with what you see, you can proceed to print. However, if you are not satisfied, you can go back to editing the document without having wasted a sheet of paper.

■   Select the <u>C</u>lose button to return to the normal view.

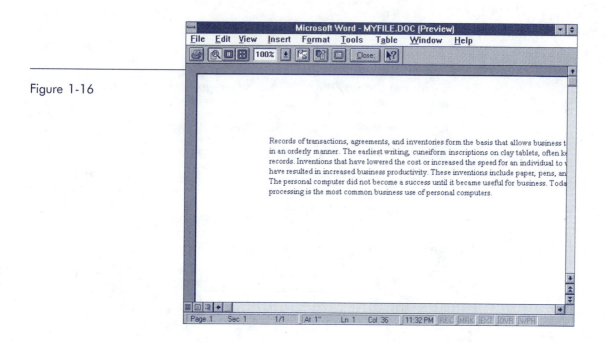

Figure 1-16

PRINTING TEXT

Now you will print the text.

■   Make sure that your printer is turned on and is ready to use.

■   From the File menu, select Print.

Alternative: **Press** Ctrl + P.

▶   *The Print dialog box is displayed, as shown in Figure 1-17.*

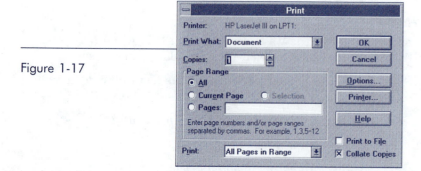

Figure 1-17

■   Make sure that the printer you are using appears next to "Printer:." If it does not, ask your instructor for help.

For now, do not change option settings.

■ Complete the command by clicking on OK or pressing Enter.

▶ *The text of MYFILE starts to print.*

NOTE: The Print tool button 🖨 gives you a convenient way to print. However, when you print using this button, the Print dialog box is not displayed.

ENDING LESSON 1

You should never quit Microsoft Word by just turning off your computer. *Always* exit to Windows and properly quit Windows before shutting down your system. When you properly exit Microsoft Word and Windows, the program will caution you if any documents have been changed since they were last saved.

■ From the File menu, select Exit.

Alternative: Press Alt + F4 .

▶ *If any open documents were changed since they were last saved, a cautionary dialog box appears, giving you a chance to save the document again. Select Yes or No accordingly. You return to Windows.*

■ Quit the Windows session.

■ Remove your data disk from the disk drive.

■ Turn off your computer and monitor.

SUMMARY

☐ **Text is entered at the position of the insertion point. The insertion point can be positioned by using the mouse.**

☐ **Uppercase letters are entered using either the Shift key or the Caps Lock key. To enter special characters that appear on the upper half of a key, the Shift key must be held down, even if the Caps Lock key has been pressed.**

☐ **Words are not split between two lines, but are placed complete on one line through a feature called *wordwrap*. Press Enter only at the end of a paragraph or to insert a blank line.**

☐ **The insertion point can be moved using the keyboard or the mouse.**

☐ **Pressing** [Ins] **toggles OVR on and off. In OVR mode, the character you type replaces the one the insertion point is on. When OVR is off, the character the insertion point is on and all characters to the right move over when text is entered.**

☐ **Text can be selected by pointing to the first character with the mouse, dragging the mouse until the text is highlighted, and releasing the mouse button. Text can also be selected using the selection bar and mouse, as well as with the keyboard.**

☐ **Selected text can be deleted, moved, or copied.**

☐ **A valid filename is one to eight characters in length, followed by an optional extension.**

☐ **When you save a file for the first time, you can enter information in the Summary Information dialog box. The information entered is used to later identify and retrieve the file.**

KEY TERMS

clipboard	insertion point	text area
dialog box	menu bar	toggle
dictionary	ruler	toolbar
drag-and-drop	selection bar	wordwrap
drop-down menu	scroll	
end mark	status bar	

COMMAND SUMMARY

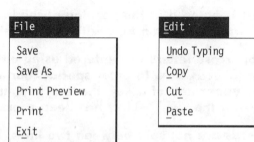

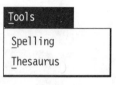

REVIEW QUESTIONS

1. Why should you not press Enter at the end of lines while entering text? When should it be pressed?
2. What keys move the insertion point without affecting the text?
3. How can you correct typing errors?
4. How do you select a word?
5. What is the purpose of the selection bar?
6. What is the purpose of tool buttons?
7. What is the maximum number of characters that can be used in a filename?
8. Describe two ways to move selected text.
9. Why do you have to save files?
10. Can the Spelling feature find all your errors? Explain.

EXERCISES

1. Enter the text below. Your document need not look exactly as it appears here.
   a. Check the spelling.
   b. Save the file as WD1EX1.
   c. Print the document.

MEMORANDUM

DATE: September 10, 1994

FROM: Lonnie Waters, Social Chairperson

SUBJECT: Fall Picnic

Don't forget to attend this year's fall picnic, to be held at the Forest Glade Regional Park on Saturday, September 24, 1994, from 11:00 a.m. to 6:00 p.m.

There will be lots of events for the entire family. We'll hold a fishing derby, and there will be races and games for all ages.

You can't beat the price: the food is free to employees and their families. Sign up by the cafeteria.

And don't forget to bring your umbrellas and rain coats, in case it rains like it did at last year's picnic.

2. Enter the text below. Your document need not look exactly as it appears here.
   a. Check the spelling.
   b. Save the file as **WD1EX2**.
   c. Print the document.

current date

Mrs. Mildred Adams, Librarian
American Historical Society
1776 Freedom Road
Philadelphia, PA

Dear Mrs. Adams:

I am writing a term paper on quotations of American presidents, focusing on their views of how government should be run. It is easy to find famous quotations for some presidents. Washington, Lincoln, both Roosevelts and Kennedy are well-represented in my research notes.

Could you help me find other noteworthy, if obscure, quotes of the presidents? I've tried Bartlett's "Quotations" and several history textbooks in the school library.

Thank you for your time and patience.

Sincerely,

Donna Lee Light

3. Enter the text below. Your document need not look exactly as it appears here.
   a. Check the spelling.
   b. Save the file as **WD1EX3**.
   c. Print the document.

Product Initiative Report:
Water Saddle

Al Jenkins, Product Development

Our department is pleased to announce its latest product invention for advanced testing and market analysis. For years, Cowpokes, Inc. has led the industry in developing innovative products for cattle ranches and rodeos. Recently, our department took a look at dude ranches, and found that

the demand is growing despite a very low return rate. One of the most frequently mentioned complaints of guests was saddle sores.

Therefore, we initiated design and preliminary testing of a revolutionary new water saddle. Like a water bed, its shape conforms to that of the rider, eliminating those bruising pressure points and reducing the tendency to slide about, causing chafing.

The water bag is double sealed in flexible but durable vinyl which simulates the look of cowhide. Preliminary testing indicates more comfort to the rider, but a need to reduce wave oscillations. We have some ideas, but this is a subject for advanced testing.

2 Formatting Documents

OBJECTIVES

Upon completion of the material presented in this lesson, you should understand the following aspects of Microsoft Word:

- ☐ **Using onscreen help**
- ☐ **Opening an existing document**
- ☐ **Recognizing the default format for printing**
- ☐ **Specifying various format options through menu commands and through the tool bars and ruler**
- ☐ **Setting margins**
- ☐ **Setting paper orientation**
- ☐ **Setting tabs and non-printing characters**
- ☐ **Setting paragraph indentation**
- ☐ **Setting line indentation**
- ☐ **Setting a hanging indent**
- ☐ **Formatting bullets**
- ☐ **Setting text alignment**
- ☐ **Centering text**
- ☐ **Setting line spacing**
- ☐ **Setting page breaks**
- ☐ **Formatting page numbering**
- ☐ **Changing font and appearance**

STARTING OFF

Turn on your computer, start Windows, and launch the Microsoft Word for Windows program as you did in the previous lesson. Insert your data disk in a disk drive. If necessary, maximize the Microsoft Word application window.

USING ONSCREEN HELP

If you have difficulty understanding or remembering a command or terminology, you can use the extensive onscreen Help system included in Microsoft Word. The onscreen Help feature of Microsoft Word is similar to Help on all Windows applications.

Let's assume right now that you do not remember how to open an existing document.

■   From the Help menu, select Contents.

Alternative: **Press the** F1 **function key.**

▶   *The Word Help Contents screen appears as shown in Figure 2-1.*

Figure 2-1

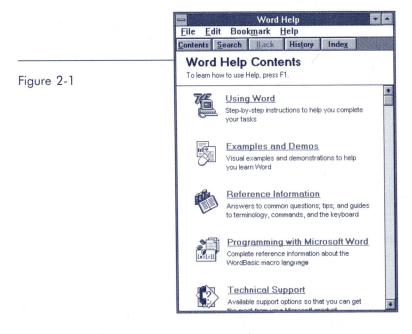

The underlined topics can be selected by clicking on them with the mouse or by pressing [Tab] or [Shift]+[Tab] to highlight the topic, then pressing [Enter].

■   Select Using Word.

▶   *A Using Word list of various features appears.*

The list of topics can be scrolled to reveal additional topics. Again, the underlined topics can be selected to reveal further information.

■   Scroll the screen to display File Management options.

■   Select "Opening, Saving, and Protecting Documents."

▶   *A further listing of related topics appears.*

■   Select "Opening an existing document."

▶   *Step-by-step instructions for opening an existing document appear.*

If you want a paper copy of this information, you can select the Print button.

■   Close the How To window by clicking on the Close button or pressing [Alt]+[F4].

Alternative: **Double-click on the control-menu box at the top left edge.**

■   Close the Word Help window by selecting the File menu, then Exit, or by pressing [Alt]+[F4].

Alternative: **Double-click on the control-menu box at the top left corner of the Help window.**

You can also do the reverse. That is, given a command, you can get an explanation of that command.

■   From the File menu, select the Open command.

▶   *The Open dialog box is displayed.*

■   Press the [F1] function key.

▶   *Information about the Open command in the File menu is displayed.*

■   Close the Help window.

■   Exit the Open dialog box by clicking on Cancel or pressing [Esc].

You can also get help on different regions of the screen, such as a tool button.

■   Press [Shift]+[F1].

▶   *The mouse pointer turns into a question mark* [?].

■ Point to the Open tool button ⬚ and click the left mouse button.

▶ *Again, the Help window describing the Open Document command is displayed.*

■ Close the Help window.

OPENING AN EXISTING DOCUMENT

Now let's open a document file. The file to open is myfile.doc, which you saved at the end of the last lesson.

■ From the File menu, select the Open command.

Alternative: Press Ctrl+O or click on the Open tool button ⬚.

▶ *A dialog box appears, as shown in Figure 2-2.*

Figure 2-2

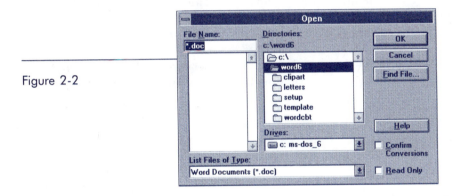

The Open dialog box looks similar to the Save As box you saw in the last lesson. It lets you specify the drive, directory, and filename of the document you want retrieved from disk. You will first specify the drive.

NOTE: If your data disk is not in drive A, substitute the appropriate drive name.

■ Click on the down arrow key at the right end of the Drives list box.

▶ *All available drives are displayed.*

■ Click on a: for drive A.

▶ *The Directories list box displays all directories currently on drive A. If you need to specify the directory, do so by clicking on the directory name.*

The File Name list box on the left displays all the files on the data disk.

■   Click on myfile.doc, then complete the command by clicking on the OK button or pressing (Enter).

▶   *The text from the previous lesson is displayed onscreen.*

FORMATTING A DOCUMENT

You may have noticed when you printed the text at the end of the last lesson that it was printed just about the way it was displayed onscreen. Because the screen display and print formats you used were preset by Microsoft Word (you were using the default settings), the document may not have been printed in the format you had in mind.

The layout and formatting of a document is affected through the page setup, paragraph format, and character appearances. Page setup includes such items as the size of the paper and the margins used—items that affect the entire document. Paragraph formats include line spacing, indentations used, and text alignment. You can also change a character's appearance using bold, underline, italics, and different fonts and character sizes.

NOTE: It is possible to divide up a document into sections and define format each section separately. You may want to explore this on your own.

PAGE SETUP

You can change the page setup through the Page Setup command in the File menu.

■   Position the insertion point anywhere in the paragraph.

■   From the File menu, select Page Setup.

▶   *The Page Setup dialog box is displayed, as shown in Figure 2-3.*

The Page Setup dialog box is composed of four different sheets: Margins, Paper Size, Paper Source, and Layout. To display a sheet, either click on the corresponding sheet tab or hold down the (Alt) key and press the underlined character of the sheet name.

Margins

Next, you will look at Margins and Paper Size.

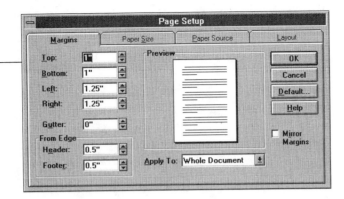

Figure 2-3

■ Select the Margins sheet, if not already displayed, by clicking on the sheet tab or pressing Alt + M.

As you can see, the default setting for top and bottom margins is 1″ and for right and left margins is 1.25″. You will now change the left margin to 2″.

■ Press the Tab key until the Left margin setting is highlighted or use the mouse to highlight the left margin setting.

■ Type **2**, then press Tab.

▶ *The Preview display on the dialog box changes to reflect the new setting.*

If you were to complete the command by clicking on OK or pressing Enter, you would return to the document with changes in effect. Right now, however, let's look at Page Size.

Paper Size

By default, the paper size selected is a standard 8½″ by 11″ and the document has the ***portrait*** orientation, as shown in the Preview display. Portrait is so named because most portraits of people are contained in frames that are taller than they are wide. A sheet printed sideways on the page is printed in ***landscape*** orientation, named because many landscapes are painted on canvases that are wider than they are high. Select paper orientation by using the radio buttons in the Orientation selection box. When a box contains radio buttons, only one button may be selected at any time, like the station selector on many automobile radios. A button is selected by clicking on it with the mouse or holding down the Alt key and pressing the underlined character in the selection name.

■ Select Paper Size.

▶ *The display changes to the one shown in Figure 2-4.*

■ Select Landscape by clicking on the radio button in front of it or by pressing Alt + C.

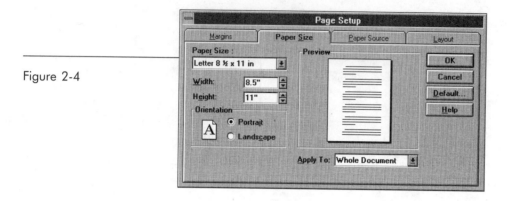

Figure 2-4

> ▶ *The Preview page display reflects the new orientation. Notice also that the Width is changed to 11".*

■ Go back to the <u>M</u>argins sheet in the dialog box.

> ▶ *The Preview page displayed here also reflects the change in orientation.*

■ Complete the command.

> ▶ *The document displayed onscreen also reflects the change in orientation. You can see that the line length is much longer.*

P R A C T I C E   T I M E   2 - 1

Change the page orientation back to Portrait.

THE RULER

At the top of the document window you see the ruler, as shown in Figure 2-5. The ruler displays the margins and custom tab settings for the paragraph that contains the insertion point.

First-line
indent marker

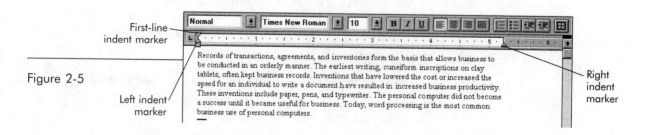

Figure 2-5

Left indent
marker

Right
indent
marker

N O T E : If the ruler is not displayed, choose Ruler from the <u>V</u>iew menu.

The numbers that are displayed along the ruler are relative to the left margin that was set using the Page Setup command. That is, 0″ is the left margin position—which, in this case, is 2″ from the left edge of the paper. In Page Setup, the paper size selected was 8½″ wide, the left margin was set to 2″, and the right margin set to 1¼″. This leaves a line length of 5¼″. This is indicated on the ruler with lighter color between 0″ and 5¼″ position.

As shown in Figure 2-5, the ruler also contains the ***first-line indent marker, left indent marker,*** and the ***right indent marker.*** These will be explained a little later.

P R A C T I C E   T I M E   2 - 2

1. From the Page Setup command, change the orientation to Landscape (this makes the paper 11″ wide). Complete the command.

2. Look at the ruler line as well as the line width of the document by using the horizontal scroll bar.

3. When satisfied, go back to the Page Setup command and change the orientation back to Portrait.

PARAGRAPH FORMATTING

If you need to change the format of just one paragraph for emphasis, position the insertion point somewhere in the paragraph and open the Format menu's Paragraph command. If you want to change the format of more than one consecutive paragraph, select them before giving the command.

Once you set the format for a particular paragraph, any paragraph that is entered below that paragraph will have the same format. That means, when you are entering a new document, if you set a format for the first paragraph, all subsequent paragraphs will have the same format. In an existing document, if you select a paragraph and change the format, other existing paragraphs will *not* be affected. If you were to insert a paragraph, that paragraph would have the format of the one that immediately precedes it in the document.

For most of these commands, there are tool buttons, ruler, and combination keystrokes that will accomplish the same task. Some require that tabs be set at appropriate positions.

TABS AND NON-PRINTING CHARACTERS

Tab settings determine the position of the insertion point each time Tab is pressed. When you press Tab, a ***non-printing*** character is inserted in the document. Hence, if you want to remove the effect of pressing Tab, you must delete the non-printing character. To make this task easier, however, you can display the non-printing character.

■   From the Tools menu, select Options.

▶   *The Options box appears as shown in Figure 2-6.*

Figure 2-6

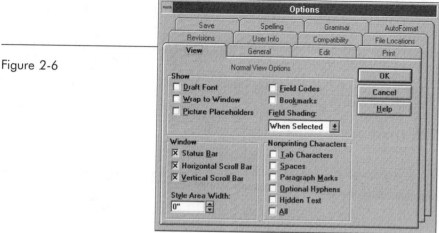

In this dialog box, you select sheets by either clicking on the sheet tab or pressing the → and ← keys.

■   Make sure that the View sheet is displayed.

■   In the non-printing Characters box, select All so that an X appears, then complete the command.

   Alternative: Click on the Show/Hide button ¶.

▶   *The document now displays ¶ where you pressed Enter. Also, dots appear where Spacebar was pressed.*

■   Position the insertion point at the end of the document, then press Enter to position the insertion point at the beginning of a new line.

■   Press Tab.

▶   *The non-printing character → appears, and the insertion point moves to the 0.5"position.*

■   Press Tab several more times.

Each time you press ⌈Tab⌉, notice the position of the insertion point. By default, tab stops are set to every half inch, starting at the left margin.

■ Press ⌈Bksp⌉ to delete tabs. Each time, notice again the position of the insertion point.

To hide the non-printing character, follow the exact same steps you used to display. That is, choose Options from the Tools menu, then click on All (so that X disappears) *or* click on the Show/Hide button.

PRACTICE TIME 2-3

1. Erase all tabs, but leave the insertion point at the beginning of a new line.

2. Hide the non-printing character.

SETTING TABS

You can insert or delete custom tabs. To add custom tab stops, select the paragraph(s) you want affected by the new tab stops, then set the tab stops. You can set the tab by using the ruler or by choosing the Tabs command from the Format menu. If you do not select specific text, tab stops are set for the paragraph that contains the insertion point. When you set a custom tab stop, Word clears all default tab stops to the left of the custom tab stop.

N O T E :   Word stores tab settings in the paragraph mark at the end of each paragraph. If you delete a paragraph mark, not only does the text become part of the following paragraph, but you delete the tab settings for that text.

■ From the Fo̲rmat menu, select T̲abs.

▶ *The Tabs dialog box, as shown in Figure 2-7, is displayed.*

Figure 2-7

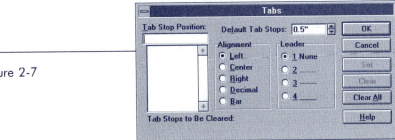

To set a tab, type the location in the Tab Stop Position text box, then select the Set button. To clear a tab, select the tab setting in the Tab Stop Position list box, then select the Clear button. To clear all tab settings, click the Clear All button.

The Alignment selection box lets you indicate the kind of tab setting. The default is left. The effects of tab types will be discussed in the next lesson. The Leader selection box is not discussed here.

Set custom tab stops at columns 1″ and 2″. Remember, tab settings are indicated relative to the left margin.

■ With the insertion bar in the Tab Stop Positions text box, type **1**, then select Set by clicking on it or pressing Alt+S.

▶ *1″ appears in the Tab Stop Position list box.*

■ Now change the entry in the Tab Stop Position text box to **2**, then select Set.

▶ *2″ appears on the Tab Stop Position list box.*

■ Complete the command.

▶ *The ruler displays custom left tab stops at 1″ and 2″ positions, and all default tab stops to the left have been cleared.*

■ Press Tab.

▶ *The insertion point is now at the 1″ position.*

■ Press Tab again.

▶ *The insertion point moves to the 2″ position.*

If you press Tab again, the insertion point will move to the next tab stop at the 2.5″ position, then to 3″, and so on. You will now delete the tab stop at 2″. This should restore the default tabs at the 1.5″ and 2″ positions.

■ From the Format menu, select Tabs to display the Tabs dialog box.

■ Select 2″ in the Tab Stop Positions list box.

■ Select Clear, then complete the command.

▶ *The custom tab stop at 2″ is cleared.*

You can also insert, remove, and move tab stops using the ruler. To set a tab, click on the ruler where you want a custom tab to be.

■ Click the ruler at the 2″ position.

▶ *A custom left tab stop is inserted.*

To get rid of any unwanted tab, drag the tab marker off the ruler.

■ Drag the custom tab stop at 2″ off the ruler.

▶ *The custom tab stop at 2″ is cleared.*

P R A C T I C E   T I M E   2 - 4

1. Set tab stops at various positions by using both the Format menu and the ruler.

2. Try pressing Tab. Display non-printing characters and look at the effect.

3. When satisfied, hide non-printing character then clear all custom tab stops (Clear All) so that default settings remain in effect.

PARAGRAPH INDENTATION

Let's say now that you want to indent an entire paragraph for emphasis. To do this, you change the values of the left and right indent for that paragraph.

■ Place the insertion point at the end of the text.

■ Insert at least one blank line by pressing Enter.

■ Type the following:

The concept behind word processing is a fascinating one. The typewriter has become archaic, stricken by a single technological blow. The concepts of training and productivity have changed, too. The more productive worker is the one who can insert text changes, make corrections, move blocks of text, and otherwise process text rewrites efficiently.

▶ *Notice that the new paragraph used the same format as the existing paragraph.*

■ Save the document as the file **myfile2** on your data disk.

You want the new paragraph to be indented.

■ Position the insertion point anywhere in the second paragraph.

■ From the Format menu, select Paragraph.

▶ *The Paragraph dialog box is displayed, as shown in Figure 2-8.*

The Paragraph dialog box is composed of two different sheets: Indents and Spacing and Text Flow. To display a sheet, either click on the corresponding sheet tab or hold down the Alt key and press the underline character of the sheet name.

■ Select Indents and Spacing, if not already displayed.

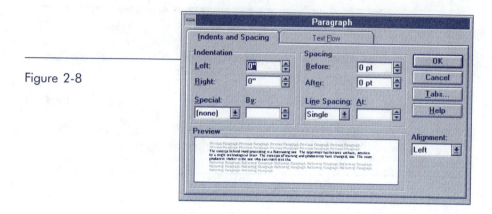

Figure 2-8

In the Preview display box at the bottom, the darker paragraph in the middle shows the format of the selected paragraph as compared to the rest of the document. At the left is the Indentation selection box.

■ In the Indentation selection box, change the Left indent to 0.75″ and press Tab.

▶ *The Preview displays the effect of the new setting on the selected paragraph.*

■ Complete the command by clicking on OK or pressing Enter.

▶ *The document display is similar to Figure 2-9.*

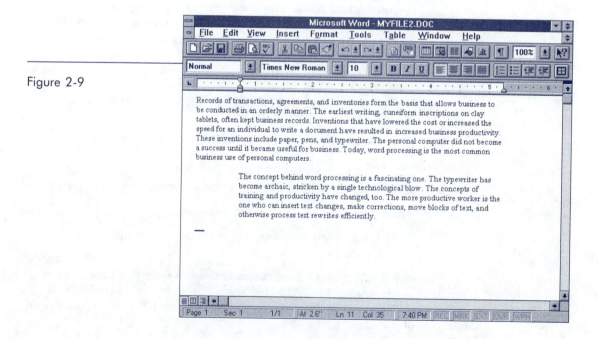

Figure 2-9

Notice the ruler line on Figure 2-9. The left indent marker and the first-line indent marker were both moved to the 0.75".

■   Position the insertion point on the first paragraph and look at the ruler line; note the position of the first-line and left indent markers.

You can indent the paragraph to the first tab stop position using a tool button.

■   With the insertion point in the first paragraph, click on the Increase Indent button 🔲.

▶   *The first paragraph is indented to the first tab stop.*

■   Click on the Increase Indent button again.

▶   *The paragraph is now indented to the second tab stop.*

Each time you click on the Increase Indent button, the paragraph indents to the next tab stop.

■   Click on the Decrease Indent button 🔲.

▶   *The indentation returns to the previous tab stop.*

P R A C T I C E   T I M E   2 - 5

Bring the first paragraph back to the left margin.

The paragraph can also be indented by dragging both the left indent marker and the first-line indent marker to the desired position. This is done by dragging the little square located just below the left indent marker.

P R A C T I C E   T I M E   2 - 6

Try setting various paragraph indentations through the Format command, tool buttons, and the ruler. When satisfied, make sure that the first paragraph is at the left margin and the second paragraph is indented 0.75".

LINE INDENTATION

Suppose you want to indent the first line of a paragraph by ½". One way you can do this, as you just learned, is to make sure that there is a tab stop at 1/2″ and then press Tab at the beginning of each paragraph. There is another way. You can set the first-line indent to 0.5″. Once the first-line indent marker is positioned, Word will indent the first line of each paragraph automatically.

- Position the insertion point anywhere in the second paragraph.

- From the Format menu, select Paragraph.

- Select Indents and Spacing, if not already displayed.

- In the Indentation selection box, click on the down arrow by the Special text box.

  ▶ *Additional options are displayed.*

- Select First Line.

  ▶ *The By text box displays 0.5″ and the Preview display shows the change.*

You can increase or decrease the width of the indentation by typing the desired amount in the By text box. Right now, you will leave it at 0.5″.

- Complete the command.

  ▶ *The first line of the second paragraph is indented 0.5″. Also, notice the position of the first-line indent marker on the ruler.*

You can set the first-line indent by dragging the first-line indent marker.

- Drag the first-line indent marker to 0.75″, the same position as the left indent marker.

HANGING INDENT

What will happen if you drag the first-line indent marker to a position to the *left* of the left indent marker? You get a **hanging indent**. In a hanging indent format, a paragraph is indented except for the first line. This format is used quite often in bibliography, such as the following:

Pitter, Keiko. *Using IBM Microcomputers.* 4th ed. Watsonville, CA: Mitchell-McGraw Hill, 1992.

You will try this just to see the effect.

- Make sure to position the insertion point in the second paragraph.

- Drag the first-line indent marker to the 0.25″ position on the ruler.

  ▶ *The first line starts at 0.25″, and the rest of the paragraph aligns at 0.75″.*

P R A C T I C E   T I M E   2 - 7

1. Drag the left-indent marker and the first-line indent marker to various positions and look at various effects.

2. When you are satisfied, add at least one blank line at the end of the document.

3. With the insertion point at the beginning of the new line, set both the left indent marker and the first-line indent marker to the 0" position. Move the right indent marker to the 3" position.

4. Enter the following text. Make sure to press Enter after each sentence.

   When a computer is instructed to do a job, it handles the task in a very special way.
   It accepts the information.
   It stores the information until the information is ready to be used.
   It processes the information.
   Then it gives out the processed information.

5. Save the file as file **FILE1.DOC**.

BULLETS

In a bulleted list, a small circle (the **bullet**) appears in front of each item on the list. In Word, the Bulleted format combines bullet with the hanging indent. For each item on the list, a bullet appears at the first-line indent marker position, and the rest of the text appears at left indent marker position.

■ Select the last four sentences entered.

■ Click on the Bullets button 📇.

▶ *The display is now bulleted, as shown in Figure 2-10.*

To clear the bullet, with the bulleted list selected, click the Bullets button again.

Figure 2-10

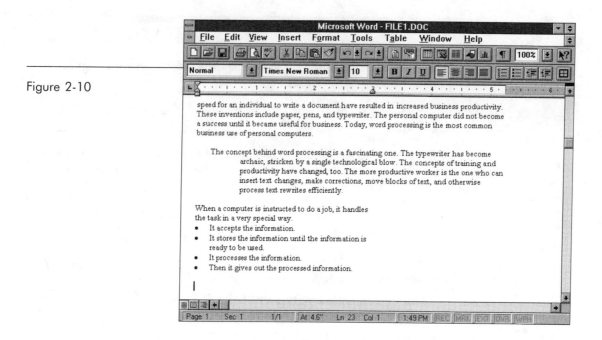

TEXT ALIGNMENT

Right now, the text is displayed aligned at the *left* margin but not at the *right* margin. You can change the alignment so that the text is aligned right, center, or justified. When the text is justified, enough blank spaces are inserted in each line so that both the left and right margins are even.

■ Position the insertion point in the first paragraph.

■ From the Format menu, select Paragraph.

▶ *The Paragraph dialog box is displayed.*

■ Make sure that the Indents and Spacing sheet is displayed.

The Alignment list box appears at the bottom right.

■ Click on the down arrow at the right end of the Alignment text box.

▶ *All four options are displayed.*

■ Select Justified and complete the command by clicking on OK or pressing [Enter].

▶ *The text reflects the change in alignment.*

This could have also been done using the buttons on the toolbar or pressing a combination keystroke. On the toolbar are four buttons for alignment, as shown in Figure 2-11. Right now, the right-most button for Justified is pressed.

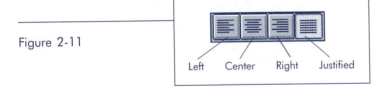

Figure 2-11

Using the combination keystroke, left alignment can be entered as Ctrl+L, right alignment as Ctrl+R, center as Ctrl+E, and justified as Ctrl+J.

■ Click on the left-most button or press Ctrl+L for left alignment.

▶ *Text is now left-aligned.*

P R A C T I C E T I M E 2 - 8

1. Select other tool buttons or press combination keystrokes for alignment and look at the result onscreen.

2. When you are satisfied, set the first paragraph to left-alignment.

CENTERING TEXT

There are times when you need to center text, such as when entering a title. Let's try it.

■ Position the insertion point at the beginning of the document.

■ Press Enter a couple of times to insert blank lines, and then place the insertion point on the first line.

■ Click on the Center button or press Ctrl+E.

▶ *The insertion point jumps to the middle of the line.*

■ Type **LESSON TITLE**.

▶ *The title is centered between the margins.*

N O T E: To center text that has already been entered, select the text, then enter the Center command.

LINE SPACING

The default setting for the line spacing is single.

■ Position the insertion point anywhere in the first paragraph.

■ From the Format menu, select Paragraph. Make sure that the Indents and Spacing sheet is displayed.

You can see the default, Single, displayed in the Line spacing text box.

■ Click on the arrow to the right of the Line Spacing text box.

▶ *All available options are displayed.*

■ Select Double.

▶ *The Preview display below shows how the document will be spaced.*

■ Complete the command by clicking on OK or pressing Enter.

▶ *The screen reflects the change in line spacing.*

P R A C T I C E   T I M E   2 - 9

1. Try selecting other options for spacing, each time looking at the Preview box.

2. When satisfied, change the spacing back to Single.

PAGE BREAKS

When you have a long, multiple-page document, Microsoft Word shows you where the printer will advance to a new page. These are known as *soft page breaks* and are shown as a horizontal line in the text onscreen.

As you look over the document, however, you may find that a soft page break occurred at some inappropriate place. For example, you do not want a page break to occur in the middle of a table, or you may want an item to be on a page all by itself. In such cases, you need to manually enter a page break, known as a *hard page break*. A hard page break is inserted by positioning the insertion point where you want the page break to occur and inserting the command for page break.

■ Place the insertion point at the end of the first paragraph.

■ From Insert menu, select Break, then complete the command.

Alternative: **Press** Ctrl + Enter.

▶ *A line is inserted after the first paragraph, as shown in Figure 2-12.*

Figure 2-12

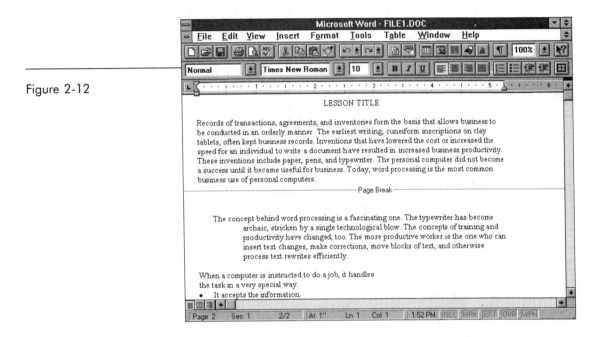

■ From the File menu, select Preview.

▶ *A page of the document is displayed.*

■ Click on the Multiple Page button 🔳 at the top.

▶ *This further selection is displayed.*

■ Drag to highlight 1 x 2, as shown in Figure 2-13.

Figure 2-13

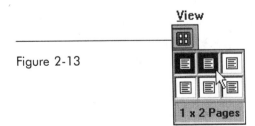

▶ *Two pages are displayed, as shown in Figure 2-14.*

You can see that the first paragraph is on one page and the rest is on the other.

Figure 2-14

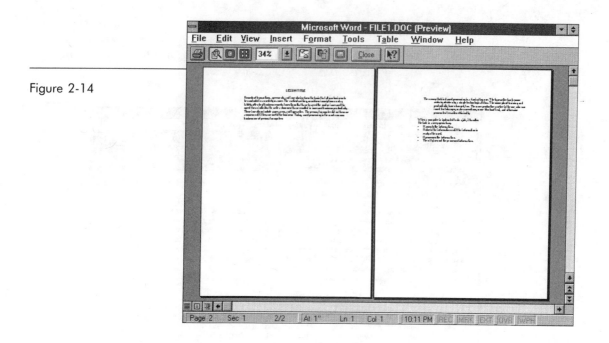

N O T E :   From this preview screen, you can print the document by clicking on the Print button.

■   Exit the Preview screen by selecting <u>C</u>lose.

Should you decide that you do not want the hard page break after all, position the insertion point just after the break and press Bksp.

PAGE NUMBERING

■   When you are creating a multiple page document, you may want to print the page number on each page.

■   Position the insertion point anywhere in the first page of the text.

■   From the <u>I</u>nsert menu, select Page Nu<u>m</u>bers.

▶   *The Page Numbers dialog box is displayed, as shown in Figure 2-15.*

You can insert a page number at the top or the bottom of the paper. The bottom is the default selection. Also, the number can appear at the left, center, or right. Right is the default selection. You will use all the default settings.

Figure 2-15

NOTE: Through the Format option, you can specify the type of numbers to such as Arab numerals (1,2,3), lowercase Roman numerals (i,ii,iii), or uppercase Roman numerals (I, II, III). You can also specify the starting number for paging.

■ Complete the command.

P R A C T I C E   T I M E   2 - 1 0

1. Preview or print the text to look at the page numbering. You may have to enlarge the display to see the page numbers.

2. Delete the hard page break.

CHANGING FONT

The appearance of characters on your screen and printout is determined by three things, which collectively are called the ***font***: the typeface, the type size, and the appearance.

The *typeface* is the design applied to the characters and given a name, such as Courier, Helvetica, or Times Roman. The typeface is often referred to as the font.

The *type size* of the character will depend on type of font. If the font you chose is **proportionally spaced** (different widths for different letters), the size is given in points, measured 72 to an inch. Typical fonts are 10- or 12-point fonts, with 10 being the smaller size. If the font you chose is **monospaced** (each letter requires the same amount of horizontal space), the size is indicated in characters per inch, or cpi. Again, the typical font sizes are 10 cpi or 12 cpi, with 12 cpi being the smaller size.

The *appearance* includes regular, bold, italic, and underline. These can be used in any combination.

You can select an appropriate font for display and printing the document. The style can be varied to emphasize certain information. The font and size will affect the amount of text that can fit on one page of a document.

To change a text font, select the text you want to change, or position the insertion point where you want to begin typing characters with the new font. If you want to change the default font selection, the insertion point can be anywhere. When you change the default setting, the entire document will use the font specified.

- ■ Select a section of the text.

- ■ From the F̲ormat menu, choose F̲ont.

  ▶ *The Font dialog box is displayed, as shown in Figure 2-16.*

Figure 2-16

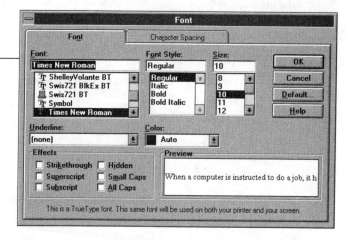

- ■ Make sure that the Font sheet is displayed.

- ■ Make a selection in the F̲ont list box.

  ▶ *The Preview display shows the font selected.*

N O T E : If you want to change the default font selection, select the Use As Default button.

- ■ When you have the desired font selected, complete the command.

  ▶ *The selected text changes to the font specified.*

You can also change the font by using the toolbar.

- ■ Click on the arrow next to the second box from the left on the Formatting toolbar.

  ▶ *The font options are displayed.*

- ■ Click on the font name you want.

Depending on the font chosen, you will have different point sizes from which to choose. Size selection is very similar to font selection; you can specify it by using the Character command from the Format menu or choosing the size (to the right of the Fonts) on the Formatting toolbar. Try this on your own.

P R A C T I C E   T I M E   2 - 1 1

Try various fonts and sizes, and study the effects.

CHANGING APPEARANCE

You can change the appearance of characters either as you type the text or after it has been typed. As mentioned earlier, appearance includes bold, underline, and italic.

To change appearance while entering text, position the insertion point where you plan to enter text, give the command to change the appearance, type the text, then give the command again to return to normal.

To change the appearance of text already typed, select the desired text, then give the command to change the appearance.

Again, the command can be given through the Font command in the Format menu or through the tool buttons. In the toolbar are three buttons, as shown in Figure 2-17, for Bold, Italic, and Underline.

Figure 2-17

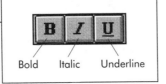

Bold   Italic   Underline

■ Position the insertion point at the end of the document.

■ Press (Enter) a couple of times to insert a blank line.

■ Click the Italic tool button or press (Ctrl)+(I).

■ Type the following:

This text is being entered in italics.

▶ *The text appears in italics onscreen.*

■ Click the Italic tool button again to return to normal characters.

Now, let's say that you want the title to appear in bold characters. Since it has already been typed, you'll have to select the text of the title, then give the Bold command.

- ■ Drag the mouse to select the text of the title.

- ■ Click the Bold tool button or press [Ctrl]+[B].

  ▶ *The title is now in bold characters.*

- ■ Click elsewhere to deselect the text.

P R A C T I C E   T I M E   2 - 1 2

Try the underline feature on your own. The combination keystroke for underline is [Ctrl]+[U].

NOTE: Once you decide on a format for selected text, the format can be copied to another section of the document by using the Format Painter tool button ⬚. All you need to do is to place the insertion point on the selected text, click on the tool button, then drag on the text where you want the same format applied. You can try this on your own.

ENDING LESSON 2

This is the end of Lesson 2. Exit Microsoft Word as explained in Lesson 1. There is no need to save changes you made to your files.

S U M M A R Y

- ☐ **Word online Help provides assistance and information on all available features.**

- ☐ **The default values set by Microsoft Word dictate how a document appears onscreen and on printouts. These values can be changed by using either the menu commands or the toolbars and the ruler.**

- ☐ **When you press [Tab], a non-printing character is inserted in the document. You can treat them like any other character. That is, if you want to delete the effect of a tab, you delete the non-printing character representing the tab.**

- ☐ **First-line indentation is when the first line of paragraph is indented. To do this, set the tab at the appropriate position and press [Tab] or set the first-line indent marker to the desired position.**

☐ **In a hanging indent, a paragraph is indented except for the first line.**

☐ **To change the font or appearance of text, you either: (1) give the command, type the text, and enter the command again; or (2) select the text, then give the command to change it.**

KEY TERMS

bullet
first-line indent marker
font
hanging indent
hard page break

landscape
left indent marker
monospaced characters
non-printing character
portrait

proportionally spaced
  characters
right indent marker
soft page break

COMMAND SUMMARY

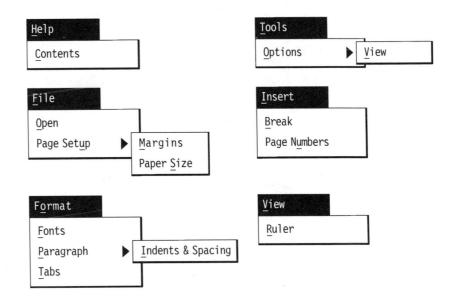

REVIEW QUESTIONS

1. What is the difference between a soft return and a hard return? a soft page break and a hard page break?

2. If you do not specify the left or right margin settings, what values are used?

3. What does "text alignment" mean? What are the options?

4. What does "hanging indent" mean? What commands do you give to use a hanging indent?

5. How do you indent an entire paragraph?

6. How do you underline characters? Make them bold?

7. What can you do from the ruler?

8. How do you set tabs using the Tabs command? Using the ruler?

9. How do you display two pages at a time during print preview?

10. List the keystrokes needed to make page numbers appear at the top right corner of each page.

EXERCISES

1. Retrieve the letter saved in the previous lesson as WD1EX2.

   a. Make the following changes, get a printout, and save it as **WD2EX1**.

   b. Center the date on the first line.

   c. Make sure that the text is left aligned.

   d. Change the left margin to 4.5" just before "Sincerely."

   e. Remove the quotation marks from the book title, "Quotations." Underline it instead.

2. Enter the following text. (Your text need not look exactly as it appears here. However, you should set new tabs before entering the recipe.)

   a. Check the spelling.

   b. Get a printout.

   c. Save it on the disk as **WD2EX2**.

Dear Jill:
I've just come across the most wonderful spaghetti sauce recipe.

1 pound	**Italian hot sausage**
1 can (4 ounces)	**sliced mushrooms, drained**
3/4 cup	**shredded carrots**
1	**medium onion, grated**
1/2 cup	**chopped parsley**
1 pound	**ground beef**
1 can (28 ounces)	**Italian style tomatoes**
2 cans (6 ounces)	**tomato paste**
1 cup	**dry red wine**
1	**bay leaf**
2 teaspoons	**salt**
1 teaspoon	**basil leaves**

1/4 teaspoon	pepper
1 pound	spaghetti

In a large pan, cook sausage in 1/4 cup water for 10 minutes, tightly covered, stirring occasionally. Remove sausage. In that pan, saute mushrooms, carrot, onion, celery and parsley in sausage drippings until crisp and tender. Remove. Add beef. Cook, stirring frequently, until lightly browned. Remove any excess fat. Return sausage and vegetables to pan. Add tomatoes, tomato paste, wine, bay leaf, salt, basil and pepper. Cover and simmer 30 minutes. Uncover and simmer 2 hours, stirring occasionally. Remove bay leaf. In the meanwhile, cook spaghetti according to directions on package. Serve with grated Parmesan cheese.

Sounds great, doesn't it? It tastes <u>delicious</u>.

Your friend,

Jackie

3. Enter the following text. Your text need not look exactly as it appears here.
   a. Check the spelling.
   b. Get a printout.
   c. Save it on the disk as **WD2EX3**.

IDEA PROCESSING

The phrases "word processing" and "data processing" are becoming more and more prevalent in common language. In the mid-1970s, who owned a word processor? What these phrases actually refer to is idea processing. With the recent growth in computer technology available to consumers, idea processing has rapidly evolved.

In many ways, idea processing has opened previously inaccessible avenues for businesses and individuals:

- Point-of-entry data terminals in a store can immediately register sales and provide data for efficient inventory and management decision.

- Financial models can show a board of directors the cold figures which, in past times, were only available <u>after</u> the decision-making had taken place.

- **Form letters no longer need to be individually typed, using so much secretarial time.**

- **Since businesses and individuals can obtain immediate access to a variety of data sets over phone lines, the possibilities for idea processing seem limited by the mind only.**

And the mind is indeed the crucial element in idea processing. For, without an accurate financial model, the best available data are worthless; without proper thought, inventory and management decisions can be detrimental to the company's well-being; without a specific and detailed method for <u>how</u> data are to be processed, access to timely data is worthless.

3 Advanced Editing and Multiple Files

OBJECTIVES

Upon completion of the material presented in this lesson, you should understand the following aspects of Microsoft Word:

- ☐ **Opening multiple documents**

- ☐ **Switching between document windows**

- ☐ **Copying selected text from one word processing file to another**

- ☐ **Inserting header and footer**

- ☐ **Entering text flush right and decimal aligned**

- ☐ **Including current date**

- ☐ **Finding a particular word or combination of words in a text**

- ☐ **Replacing a particular word or combination of words in a text with a specified word or combination of words**

- ☐ **Using merge**

STARTING OFF

Turn on your computer, start Windows, and launch the Word program as you did in previous lessons. Insert your data disk in the disk drive. If necessary, maximize the Word application window.

OPENING MULTIPLE FILES

As was mentioned in Lesson 1, you can open up to nine documents at the same time in Word if your computer has enough memory. You will now open two files from your data disk: MYFILE and FILE1.

P R A C T I C E   T I M E   3 - 1

1. Open the file MYFILE.DOC on your data disk.

2. Open the file FILE1.DOC on your data disk.

You can see only the content of FILE1.DOC onscreen right now.

Switching Between Windows

You can switch between or among document windows through the Window menu.

- ■ Select <u>W</u>indow in the menu bar.

  ▶ *The pull-down menu appears, as shown in Figure 3-1.*

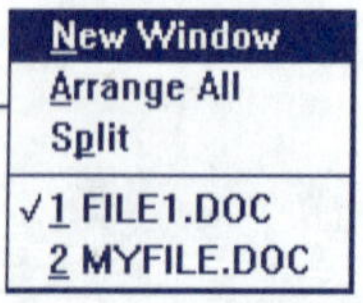

Figure 3-1

<u>N</u>ew Window
<u>A</u>rrange All
S<u>p</u>lit
√<u>1</u> FILE1.DOC
<u>2</u> MYFILE.DOC

The two documents appear as command options. You can select which document to make **active**. The active window contains the document with which you can work. In the Window menu, the active document has a check mark in front of it.

- ■ Select 2, the number that appears in front of MYFILE.

  ▶ *The document MYFILE is made active.*

PRACTICE   TIME   3 - 2

Make the document FILE1 active.

Arranging Windows

You can also switch active documents by displaying both documents at the same time.

■   From the <u>W</u>indow menu, select <u>A</u>rrange All.

▶   *The two open windows reduce in size so that they can both be viewed in the workspace, as shown in Figure 3-2.*

Figure 3-2

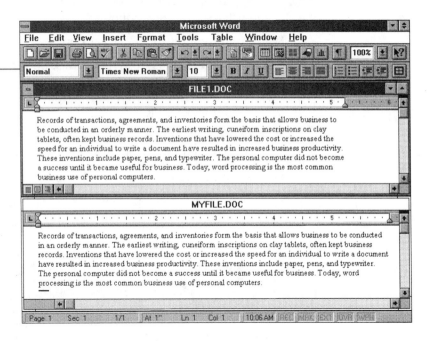

The active window is the one in which the insertion point appears and that has a darker title bar. To make a document window active, click anywhere in the window. You can also maximize the window so that it is the only document window in the display.

■   Click anywhere in the other document window.

▶   *The MYFILE document is now the active window.*

PRACTICE   TIME   3 - 3

Maximize the FILE1 document window.

WP60 Lesson 3 — Advanced Editing and Multiple Files

MOVING SELECTED TEXT BETWEEN DOCUMENTS

Sometimes you need to take a passage of text from one document and insert it into another. In Word, moving selected text between two documents is no different than moving it within a document. You cut or copy selected text onto Windows' clipboard, then paste it.

You will select the second paragraph of FILE1 so that it can be included in MYFILE.

■ Select the second paragraph of FILE1.

The selected text can be cut or copied. When you cut, the text is no longer at the original location. When the selected text is copied, however, the original stays intact. Since you do not want to remove this paragraph from FILE1, you will use the copy option.

■ From the Edit menu, select Copy.

Alternative: Press Ctrl+C or click on the Copy button 🖸.

▶ *The selected text is copied onto the clipboard.*

■ Switch to MYFILE.

■ Position the insertion point at the end of the document. Press Enter twice to insert a blank line.

■ From the Edit menu, select Paste.

Alternative: Press Ctrl+V or click on the Paste button 🖸.

▶ *The selected text is inserted as shown in Figure 3-3.*

Figure 3-3

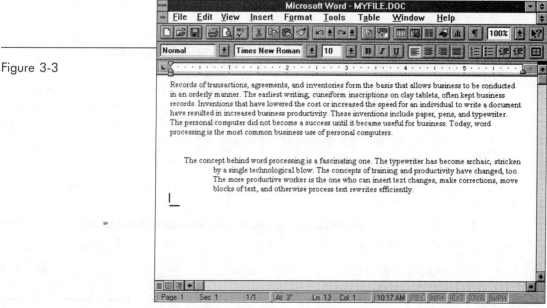

NOTE: If both documents are on display (Arrange All), you can even use the drag and drop feature to copy or move the text between files.

OPENING A NEW DOCUMENT

You will now open a new document.

■   From the File menu, select New.

Alternative: **Press** [Shift]+[N].

▶   *The New dialog box appears as shown in Figure 3-4.*

Figure 3-4

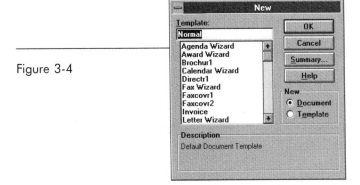

Every Word document is based on a document ***template***, which is a special document used as a pattern to create other documents of the same type. For example, you can create a document template for letters that makes it easy to produce letters of the same format. When you use a template, you no longer have to start from scratch each time you create a document. Tasks such as setting the margins, choosing a font, and creating headers and footers have already been done. Microsoft Word comes with several predefined templates for the most common types of documents. By default, new documents are based on a template called NORMAL.DOT. You can explore other templates on your own.

■   Use the default template selection and complete the command.

▶   *A document window appears.*

P R A C T I C E   T I M E   3 - 4

1. Copy the first paragraph from MYFILE to the new document just created.

2. Arrange all documents.

3. Maximize the FILE1 document.

HEADERS AND FOOTERS

Headers and ***footers*** are lines of text that appear at the top and bottom of every page. They are handy options for displaying information identifying a document. You need to enter these commands only once; the headers or footers will be repeated as specified, starting with the page on which the command was given.

The manner in which headers and footers are specified is similar. Here, only the footer is discussed. You can try the header on your own.

■ Place the insertion point at the beginning of the page.

■ From the <u>V</u>iew menu, select <u>H</u>eader and Footer.

▶ *The display switches to **page layout view** and displays the Header and Footer toolbar as shown in Figure 3-5.*

Figure 3-5

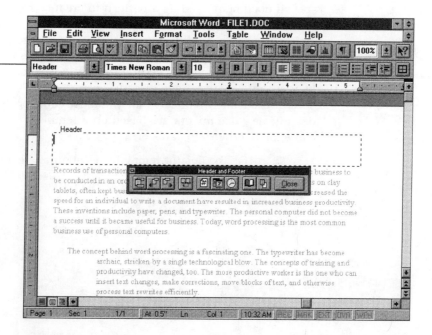

Up to now, your document was being displayed in the normal view. Word was displaying what your text would look like. In page layout view, however, you can see exactly what the document will look like when printed—similar to the Print Preview screen. Whereas in the Print Preview screen, entire pages are displayed at reduced size, the page layout view is similar in size to the normal view. You can switch between normal view and page layout view in the View menu or by clicking on the Normal View and Page Layout View buttons ▤▣ next to the horizontal scroll bar.

Notice the dotted box labeled Header. All you need to do is to type the text to appear as the header.

■ Type the following, but do not press Enter at the end.

Lesson on Advanced Editing - Page

The idea is to display the current page number at this point.

■ Click on the Page Number tool button ▣ in the Header and Footer toolbar.

▶ *Number 1 appears in the header. This is the current page number.*

■ Select Close in the Header and Footer toolbar.

P R A C T I C E   T I M E   3 - 5

1. Insert a hard page break after the first paragraph so that this becomes a multiple-page document.

2. Preview the document to see both pages. The header on the second page indicates Page 2.

CLOSING DOCUMENTS

Closing the document removes the active document from memory without exiting Word. Right now, you want to close all three documents. Each document must be closed individually.

■ From the File menu, select Close.

▶ *A dialog box appears asking you if you want to save the file or cancel the command.*

■   Select <u>N</u>o.

▶   *The document is closed (cleared) without being saved, and another open document becomes active.*

PRACTICE TIME 3-6

1.   Close the other two documents without saving changes.

2.   Open a new document using the Normal template.

ENTERING TEXT RIGHT ALIGNED

Most of the time, you enter text starting at the left margin. That is, other than line indentation, you want your lines at the left margin. If you also want the text to be even at right margin, you turn the alignment to justified. There are times, however, when you want the text to be entered aligned with the right margin, without regard to the left margin. An example might be when you are entering the date at the beginning of a letter.

■   From the F<u>o</u>rmat menu, select <u>P</u>aragraph. Then set the Alignment to Right and complete the command.

Alternative: **Press Ctrl+R or click on the right alignment tool button.**

▶   *The insertion point moves to the right margin.*

■   Type ***current date*** and press Enter.

▶   *The text is entered right aligned—even with the right margin.*

PRACTICE TIME 3-7

Set the alignment to left.

INCLUDING THE CURRENT DATE

Your computer keeps track of time when it is on. If you do not have a battery-operated clock (which stays on when the computer is turned off), you have the option to enter the current date and time when you start up the computer. Nevertheless, there is an internal clock that keeps time and date information. You can have Word insert the current date (as kept by the internal clock) into the document.

■ From the Insert menu, select Date and Time.

▶ *The Date and Time dialog box appears as shown in Figure 3-6.*

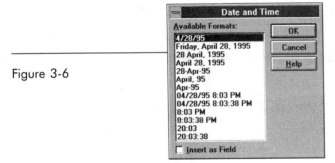

Figure 3-6

The Available Formats box lists all the different ways in which date and time can be displayed.

■ Click on the format you want, say, the fourth one down, and complete the command.

▶ *The current date is inserted at the insertion point in the format you selected.*

NOTE: Note the option to Insert as Field at the bottom of the Date and Time dialog box. When this option is selected, Word inserts the date or time as a field code, which it updates at printing. Also, if the date and time are inserted as a field code, you can update as you work by positioning the insertion point in the date or time and clicking the right mouse button, then choosing the option Update Field in the menu that is displayed.

P R A C T I C E   T I M E   3 - 8

1. Close the current document window without saving.

2. Start a new document and enter the partial letter shown following. The first address and the date are to be entered flush right.

1728 Forest Road

Takoma Park, Maryland

current date

Mr. Gary Bradshaw

Computer Parts Shop

1234 Byte Street

Golden, Colorado 81234

Dear Mr. Bradshaw:

Please accept my order for the following items:

3. Save the text on your data disk as LETTER1.

TAB ALIGNMENT

In the letter you started in Practice Time 3-8, the next step is to specify the items you want to order, the quantity, and the price, as shown below:

50	boxes of diskettes @14.75	$737.50
5	printer ribbons @11.95	59.75
1	diskette container @9.95	9.95

The first column is typed right aligned (at a specific position, +1" in this case), the second column is typed left aligned (at another specific position, +1.5" in this case), and the third column needs to be aligned at the decimal point (at position +5" in this case). You can set the tabs so that this type of data entry is simple.

- ■ Make sure that the insertion point is at the bottom of the letter. (There should be at least one blank line after the end of the text.)

- ■ From the Format menu, select Tabs.

  ▶ *The Tabs dialog box is displayed.*

You will set tabs at +1″, +1.5″, and +5″. However, at +1″, you want to specify right alignment; at +1.5″, left alignment; and at +5″, decimal alignment.

■ Click on <u>R</u>ight in the Alignment box, type **1** in the Tab Stop Position text box, then click on <u>S</u>et.

■ Click on <u>L</u>eft in the Alignment box, type **1.5** in the Tab Stop Position text box, then click on <u>S</u>et.

■ Click on <u>D</u>ecimal in the Alignment box, type **5** in the Tab Stop Position box, then click on <u>S</u>et.

■ Complete the command.

▶ *The ruler appears as shown in Figure 3-7.*

Figure 3-7

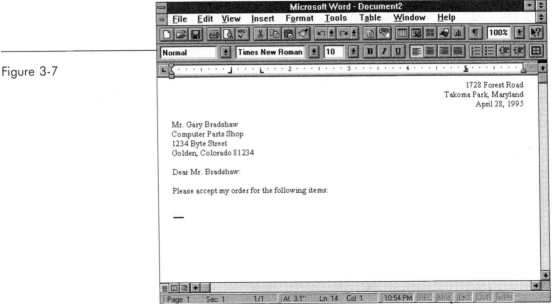

To specify various types of tabs on the ruler, click on the tab style box located at the left end of the ruler. Each time you click, the icon for tab style changes. To set a left tab, make sure that the icon for the left tab is displayed, then click on the ruler at the desired position. To set a right tab, first you make sure that the icon for the right tab is displayed before clicking on the ruler, and so on.

Now you are ready to enter the text.

■ Press ⌈Tab⌉.

▶ *The insertion point jumps to the first tab setting.*

■ Type **50**.

▶ *The entry is made flush right at position +1″.*

■   Press [Tab].

▶   *The insertion point jumps to position +1.5".*

■   Type **boxes of diskettes @14.75**.

▶   *The entry is made left justified at position +1.5".*

■   Press [Tab].

▶   *The insertion point jumps to position +5".*

■   Type **$737.50**.

▶   *The entry is made with the decimal point at position +5".*

■   Press [Enter].

P R A C T I C E   T I M E   3 - 9

1. Type in the next two items.

2. Insert a blank line after the third item.

3. Reset the tabs so that they appear every 0.5". (Hint: select Clear <u>A</u>ll in the Tabs dialog box or drag custom tabs off the ruler line.)

4. Enter the rest of the letter.

   My check for $807.20 is enclosed.

   Sincerely,

   your name

   Enclosure

5. Save the text again, using the same filename.

6. Close the file **letter1**.

FINDING TEXT

There are times when you need to move the insertion point to a specific word that you know is somewhere in the document. Microsoft Word has a command to help you do just that. You can search from the insertion point forward or backwards in a document.

■   Open the file MYFILE from your data disk.

Pretend that this is a long document on record management, and you need to find the word "cuneiform" because you have additional information you want to insert.

■ From the Edit menu, select Find.

Alternative: Press Ctrl + F.

▶ *The Find dialog box appears as shown in Figure 3-8.*

Figure 3-8

In the Find What box, you need to enter the text you want to find. You can type up to 255 characters in the Find What box. Text scrolls horizontally in the box as you type.

The Search list box shows that you are to search the entire document (All). If you were to press the down arrow at the end of the Search list box, you will see the other two search options.

■ Click the down arrow at the right end of the Search list box.

▶ *You see the options Down and Up.*

Down search means the search is made down the document from the current position of the insertion point, and up search means the search is made from the current insertion point position toward the beginning of the document.

■ Leave the selection at All.

If you do not select Match Whole Word Only, Word will find text that is part of another word. For example, you might be searching for the last name "Thorn," and Word will locate "Thornapple" as well.

If you do not select Match Case, the search is not case sensitive. That is, the text is matched with both upper- and lowercase occurrences within the document. If you select Match Case, however, the search is case sensitive. Microsoft Word looks for an exact match.

Other options are not discussed here.

■ In the Find What box, type **cuneiform**, then select Find Next.

▶ *The first occurrence of the word "cuneiform" is highlighted.*

■ Click on Cancel to close the Find dialog box.

P R A C T I C E   T I M E   3 - 1 0

Find all occurrences of the word "productivity" in MYFILE. (When you initiate the search, the word "cuneiform" still appears in the Find What box. Just type "productivity." It will replace the previous entry.)

REPLACING WORDS

In the course of editing a document, sometimes you are looking for a particular word that needs to be replaced. For example, you had written a rather lengthy report on a client only to find out that there has been a change in the client's company name. Rather than searching through the entire document visually, looking for any occurrence of the company name and replacing the name, you'd like Word to find and replace them for you.

P R A C T I C E   T I M E   3 - 1 1

1. Open a new document. Enter the following text, date the letter and add an appropriate closing, then save as the file LETTER2.

    Mr. John Smith

    Personnel Office, Republic Engineering

    3570 Fruitland Avenue

    Maywood, OR 97119

    Dear Mr. Smith:

    This is a letter of application for the draftsperson position advertised by Republic Engineering. As you will notice in the enclosed resume, my background is just what Republic Engineering is looking for.

    Please notice also that I have twice been selected as employee of the month in my current job. Republic Engineering is surely interested in my loyal attitude toward my employer.

    I look forward to hearing from you concerning an interview date and time. In the meanwhile, could you provide me with some information concerning the medical and retirement benefits available to Republic Engineering employees?

    Thank you.

You just found out that Mr. John Smith is no longer with Republic Engineering. The letter has to be sent to Mr. John Matthews.

■ From the Edit menu, select Replace.

Alternative: **Press** Ctrl + H.

▶ *The Replace dialog box, as shown in Figure 3-9, is displayed.*

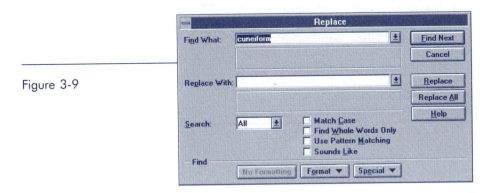

Figure 3-9

First, you need to specify the character string you want to find.

■ With the insertion point in the Find What text box, type **Smith** (do not press Enter).

Next, you need to specify with what to replace "Smith."

■ Position the insertion point in the Replace With text box.

■ Type **Matthews**.

■ Make sure that the Search text box is set to All.

As you did with the Find command earlier, you must indicate whether to match whole words only or not, and whether you want to do a case-sensitive search. You will leave these unselected.

You have the options of selecting the Find Next button or Replace All button. If you select the Replace All button, you can have all occurrences of "Smith" replaced with "Matthews" without being asked at each occurrence. With the Find Next button, Word will pause after finding the next occurrence.

■ Select the Find Next button to start the search.

▶ *The first occurrence of "Smith" is highlighted.*

■ Select the Replace button.

▶ *"Smith" is replaced with "Matthews," and the next occurrence of "Smith" is found.*

■ Keep on confirming the replacement until all occurrences of "Smith" have been replaced by "Matthews." You will know this is done when no more text is selected.

■ Close the Replace dialog box.

P R A C T I C E   T I M E   3 - 1 2

1. Replace all occurrences of "Republic Engineering" with "Conway Architects" without confirming.

2. Save the letter as **A:LETTER3**.

3. Close all documents.

MERGE

Replace is a good command to use if you are just substituting one phrase with another (or several phrases with several other phrases) one time only. However, if you need to do this many times, such as when sending the same letter to different persons, you should be using the **Merge** command instead.

The letter or the document itself, called the **main document**, needs to be modified to contain the codes where names and addresses should be inserted. Names and addresses, or whatever other information should be merged into the main document, are entered in a separate file, referred to as the **data source**. The command will then "merge" two files to create as many merged documents as there are sets of information in the data source, with the proper information inserted at indicated positions.

These two files can be created in whatever order you want. What does matter is that the order in which information is supplied in the data source match up with the codes in the main document. Right now, you will create the data source first, then create the main document.

The following letter is the one you want to send out.

---

current date

Sam Sherman
3983 West Blvd.
Los Angeles, CA 90016

Dear **Sam:**

If you need $2000 worth of equipment right away, it's a
serious matter. And borrowing money to make the
purchase is not always easy. But because you, **Sam**, have
a good credit rating with us, you are now preapproved for
a $2000 credit limit.

If you are interested, give us a call and one of our sales
people will visit you in your fair city of **Los Angeles** right
away. Also, if you need more than the $2000 credit limit,
Sam, please let us know. We'll go out of our way to help
you any way we can.

Sincerely,

In the letter, all text in bold is personalizing information. The idea is to
create as many copies of this letter as you have names and addresses in the
data source, all personalized. That means, within the letter, you need to
specify where to insert first name, where to insert address, city, and so
forth.
   You will next use the Mail Merge command.

■   From the File menu, select New.

   ▶   *The New dialog box appears.*

■   Click on OK or press Enter.

■   From the Tools menu, select Mail Merge.

   ▶   *The Mail Merge Helper dialog box appears as shown in*
       Figure 3-10.

■   Select Create.

   ▶   *A menu appears with various types of main documents you*
       might want to create.

■   Select Form Letters.

Figure 3-10

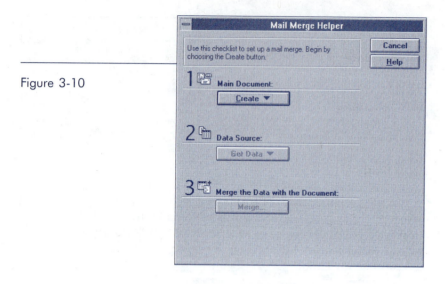

> ▶ *A dialog box appears, giving you the option to create the form letter in the document window you've already opened (active window) or in a new document window.*

■ Select <u>A</u>ctive Window.

> ▶ *You return to the Mail Merge Helper window.*

Data Source

The next step is to create a data source.

■ Select <u>G</u>et Data.

> ▶ *You have options to create a data source or open an existing one.*

> ▶ *Select <u>C</u>reate Data Source.*

> ▶ *The Create Data Source dialog box is displayed, as shown in Figure 3-11.*

Figure 3-11

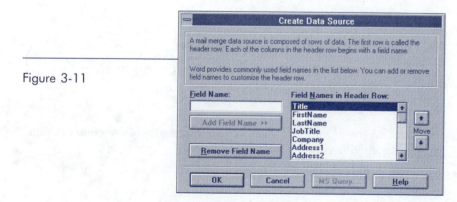

The data you enter is organized into data records in a table. The *field* names appear in the first row of cells, the header record, and act as column headings for the address information. All information related to a person appears in a row and is referred to as a **record**. Each record contains fields: a field that contains first name, a field that contains last name, a field that contains street address, and so on. All records in a data file must contain the same fields, listed in the same order.

The first step in creating a new data source is to decide which information you want to vary in each version of the merged document. For the current exercise, you need fields for the following: first name, last name, company, street address, city, state, and zip code.

The next step is to specify the field names to be used. In the Create Data Source dialog box, Word provides commonly used field names in the Field Names in Header Row list box. All you need to do is to add to or remove from the list. If you want to add new field names, a field name can be up to 32 characters. You can use letters, numbers, and underscored characters, but not spaces.

Scroll through the list. The list contains all the field names you need; you just have to remove some.

- Select Title in the Field Names in Header Row list box, then select <u>R</u>emove Field Name.

- Similarly, remove other fields so that the only ones left are: FirstName, LastName, Company, Address1, City, State, and PostalCode.

- When finished, complete the command.

  ▶ *The Save Data Source dialog box appears so that you can save the data file.*

- Save it as **Customer** on your data disk.

  ▶ *A dialog box appears, giving you the option to enter new records in the data source.*

- Select Edit <u>D</u>ata Source.

  ▶ *The Data Form dialog box appears, as shown in Figure 3-12, ready to accept information.*

Figure 3-12

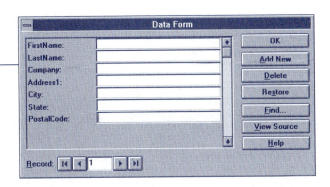

The first record contains information on Kay Gray of Buttons & Banners. The address is P.O. Box 2110, Incline Village, NV 89450.

■   Type the first field of the first record. That is, type **Kay** and press Tab.

■   Type the second field, **Gray**, and press Tab.

■   Enter the other five fields. Make sure to press Tab after each.

Company:	**Buttons & Banners**
Address1:	**P.O. Box 2110**
City:	**Incline Village**
State:	**NV**
PostalCode:	**89450**

■   After you've entered the last field, select <u>A</u>dd New.

▶   *A blank form appears.*

P R A C T I C E   T I M E   3 - 1 3

Enter the information on four other customers. If a field does not contain information (such as no company name given), just press Tab.

George Biehl
Language Technologies
2451 Vegas Valley Drive
Las Vegas NV 89121

Dorothy Durkee
Casino Computers
1255 W. Second Street
Reno NV 89502

Ronald Foss
Heritage Product
P.O. Box 320
Minden NV 89423

Ressa Muller

3000 S. State St.
Ukiah CA 95482

■   When you've finished entering the data, complete the command.

▶   *The document window for the main document appears, as shown in Figure 3-13. It includes buttons you need to merge field codes.*

You may want to position the mouse pointer over various merge buttons and find out what they do.

Main Document

The first thing you need to type is the name (first and last names) of the person to whom you are writing, followed by the company name one line

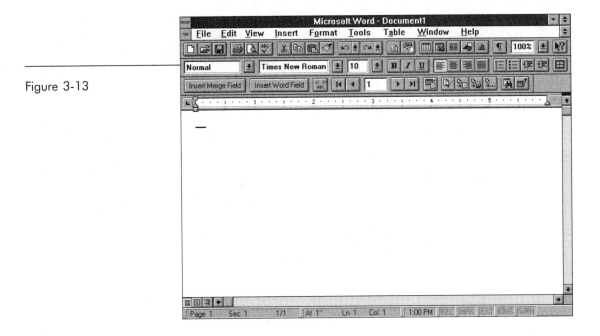

Figure 3-13

down, street address, then the city/state/zip on the next line down. This information has to come from the data file.

- ■   Insert today's date and press ⌕Enter⌗ three times.

- ■   Select Insert Merge Field.

    ▶   *A drop-down menu appears, listing all available fields, as shown in Figure 3-14.*

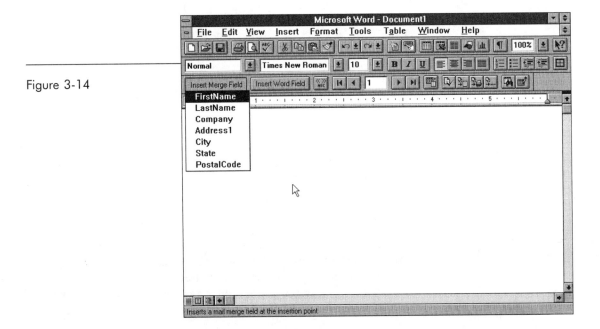

Figure 3-14

■ Select the FirstName field in the Print Merge Fields list box.

▶ *The code <<FirstName>> is inserted in the document.*

When entering field codes into a document, these codes are treated as if they were actual words or blocks of text. Any spacing or punctuation you would normally place in the text should be inserted around the code. Here, for example, you want a blank space between the first name and the last name. Hence, you need to place a space between the two codes.

■ Press (Spacebar).

■ Select Insert Merge Field and select LastName.

▶ *The line now reads <<FirstName>> <<LastName>>.*

■ Press (Enter) to move the insertion point to the next line down.

The second line prints the company name, which constitutes the third field.

■ Select Insert Merge Field, then Company.

■ Press (Enter) to go to the next line.

■ Similarly, enter Address1 on the next line down; and City, State, and PostalCode on the one after. Remember to insert a comma after the City field.

▶ *The screen should look as follows:*

<<FirstName>> <<LastName>>

<<Company>>

<<Address1>>

<<City>>, <<State>> <<PostalCode>>

Next, you need to insert a blank line, then the salutation should be entered.

■ Press (Enter) twice.

■ Type **Dear** and press (Spacebar), but do not press (Enter).

To make the letter personal, you will insert the customer's first name here.

■ Enter the merge code for FirstName, followed by a colon. Press (Enter).

■ Enter the following text. Insert the proper merge code wherever you see <FirstName> or <City>.

If you need $2,000 worth of equipment right away, it's a serious matter. And borrowing money to make the purchase is not always easy. But because you, <FirstName>, have a good credit rating with us, you are now preapproved for a $2,000 credit limit.

If you are interested, give us a call and one of our sales people will visit you in your fair city of <City> right away. Also, if you need more than the $2,000 credit limit, <FirstName>, please let us know. We'll go out of our way to help you any way we can.

Sincerely,

■   Save the file as **MAINDOC** on your data disk.

You can now begin the merging procedure. This is where the information from the data file is merged into the main document. Microsoft Word will create five letters as there are five records in the data file.

■   From the <u>T</u>ools menu, select Mail Merge.

Alternative: Click on the Mail Merge button [image].

■   Select <u>M</u>erge.

▶   *The Merge dialog box is displayed as shown in Figure 3-15.*

Figure 3-15

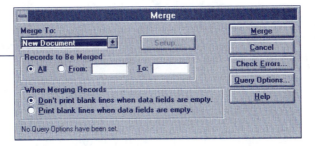

■   Select Me<u>r</u>ge To by clicking on the down arrow at the right or pressing **R.**

You have two options in merging: (1) You can merge the main document and data source, and print each resulting merged document; or (2) You can merge the main document and data source, and store the resulting documents in a new file.

The second is the default, which you will use.

If you recall, the fifth record, the one on Ressa Mueller, did not contain the Company name. To eliminate the blank line caused by an empty field, make sure that <u>D</u>on't print blank lines when data fields are empty is selected.

NOTE: You could have used either the Merge to Document button or the Merge to Printer button on the Merge toolbar. The task would have been completed using all the default settings.

■   Select <u>M</u>erge.

▶   *Each form letter appears as a document, as shown in Figure 3-16.*

Figure 3-16

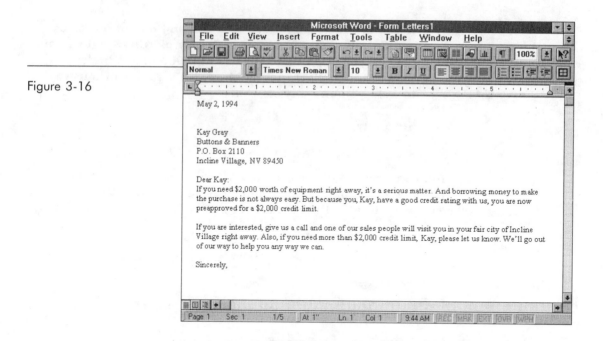

Scroll through the form letters. Notice the fifth letter to Ressa Muller. The blank line (for company name) is eliminated.

You can print these five letters or save the letters as a file. As you can imagine, the information you can merge in a letter is not just limited to mailing information. You can include account balance, due dates, or any other information that needs to be personalized. To include this information, make sure it appears in the data file.

ENDING LESSON 3

This is the end of Lesson 3. Exit Microsoft Word as explained in Lesson 1. There is no need to save changes you made to your file.

SUMMARY

☐ **By using the Arrange All command from the Window menu, all document windows are reduced in size and displayed in windows.**

☐ **Copying selected text from one file to another is done with the same procedure as is copying selected text within a file.**

☐ **Headers and footers are lines of text that appear at the top and bottom of every page.**

☐ **The current date, as kept by the computer, can be inserted in a document.**

☐ **Text can be entered flush right, left justified, or decimal aligned at each tab set.**

☐ **In Find or Replace, the text can be scanned in either direction starting from the insertion point.**

☐ **Merge requires two files. The first, the main document, contains the form document, along with all codes necessary to tell Microsoft Word what information is to be merged. The second file, a data source, contains records of data that are to be merged into the primary file.**

KEY TERMS

active window   header   record
data source   main document   template
field   merge
footer   page layout view

COMMAND SUMMARY

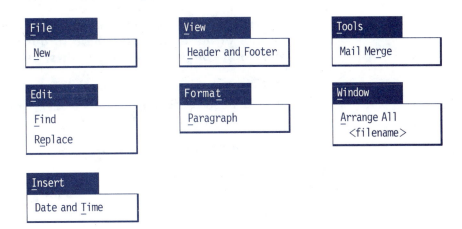

File	View	Tools
New	Header and Footer	Mail Merge

Edit	Format	Window
Find	Paragraph	Arrange All
Replace		<filename>

Insert
Date and Time

REVIEW QUESTIONS

1. What is the purpose of arranging windows?

2. What is the difference between the Cut and Copy commands?

3. What does "right align" mean? How do you enter text aligned right?

4. What does "decimal align" mean? How do you enter numbers with decimal alignment?

5. What is the difference between a normal view and a page layout view?

6. How do you enter the current date in the document?

7. In a find or replace, how do you make search case sensitive?

8. In a find or replace, what happens if you select "Match Whole Word Only"?

9. In Merge, how do you automatically eliminate blank lines for a field that is empty?

10. What are the two files needed in Merge? Explain the purpose of each file.

EXERCISES

1. Enter the following memo. (This exercise also requires you to copy information from the file WP2EX2.)

   MEMORANDUM

   DATE: *current date*

   TO: **All Employees**

   FROM: **Barbara Pettway**

   SUBJECT: **Recipe Contest Winner**

   Jackie Copeland, of the Finance Office, was selected the winner of the food contest held at our annual fall picnic. The following spaghetti recipe won first prize of $25.

   a. Copy the recipe from file WD2EX2 here.

   b. Add the following to ingredients at an appropriate location.

   1/2 cup diced celery
   Parmesan cheese

   c. Check the spelling.

   d. Save the file on the disk as file **WP3EX1**.

   e. Print the letter.

2. Enter the following memo. (This exercise also requires you to copy information from the file WP1EX3 to paste into this document.)

   MEMORANDUM

   DATE: *current date*

   TO: **Market Analysis Department**

   FROM: **Charles Jackson, President**

   SUBJECT: **Water Saddle**

Al Jenkins of Research has come up with a water saddle which shows some promise.

a. Copy the block of text from WP1EX3, beginning with "Recently, our department ..." and ending with " ... causing chafing." Indent both paragraphs 0.5".

b. Add the following:

Please look into the dude ranch market and provide an estimate for product orders over each of the next five years.

c. Check the spelling.

d. Save the file on the disk as **WP3EX2**.

e. Print the memo.

3. Create the following report.

a. Check the spelling.

b. Save as **WP3EX3**.

c. Print the report.

CHILD-WATCH SERVICES COMPANY
TRIAL BALANCE
current date

Cash (111)	$1,780	
Accounts Receivable (112)	1,600	
Equipment (141)	990	
Buses (143)	7,400	
Notes Payable (211)		$7,000
Accounts Payable (212)		1,470
Janet Escamilla, Capital (311)		3,300
	$11,770	$11,770

4 Graphics, Columns, Templates, and Tables

OBJECTIVES

Upon completion of the material presented in this lesson, you should understand the following aspects of Microsoft Word:

☐ **Inserting a border**

☐ **Creating newspaper-style columns**

☐ **Inserting a graphic picture**

☐ **Using a template**

☐ **Creating a table**

STARTING OFF

Turn on your computer, start Windows, and launch the Microsoft Word program as you did in previous lessons. Insert your data disk in disk drive. If necessary, maximize the Word application window.

You will learn the use of columns and graphic pictures by creating a newspaper-style document. Newspaper-style documents have multiple columns on a single page. Text flows from column to column. That is, as you enter text, it fills the first column, then the next column on the same page. When the last column on the page is full, text starts to fill the first column on the next page. When you add or delete text in any of the columns, the remaining text adjusts to keep the columns full. In addition, a newspaper-style document usually has a heading at the top of the first page, and some graphic pictures included in the story.

You will create a newsletter for Sierra Loma Homeowners Association as shown in Figure 4-1.

Figure 4-1

SIERRA LOMA LOG

Newsletter for Sierra Loma Homeowners Association

October, 1995

HOSE BIBS
Many residents have not disconnected their hoses from the outside hose bib since we have had such warm weather. The hose will act as a vacuum and trap the water inside the faucet extension behind the wall. When the water freezes and expands, the pipe may crack under the pressure of the ice. Then when the hose is used, the water runs under your house or into the wall causing substantial damage. Please disconnect your hoses. Should you have a problem, the Association will not be responsible for either the repair to the hose bib or the resulting damage to your home.

HEAT IN UNOCCUPIED UNITS
 If your unit is left vacant, it is important to leave enough heat so as to prevent your water pipes from freezing. Any subsequent damage resulting from frozen pipes will be the homeowner's responsibility, and not subject to insurance claims.

WINDOW WASHING
The Association has had several inquiries as to homeowners wanting their windows washed. The Association does not provide this service. If you check the Yellow Pages, there are several licensed and insured companies available.

MAINTENANCE AND LANDSCAPE
There will be a "skeleton" maintenance crew from November 1, 1995, through March, 1996. Should, if, or when we

have snow, they will be shoveling it from the walks. For your safety, please do not use salt of any kind on the sidewalks. The snow melts when the salt is applied, and refreezes to a slick, icy, and dangerous condition. If you have an area needing "special attention," contact Fred Leisler, maintenance supervisor, at 747-7600.

ASSOCIATION DUES
The monthly homeowners dues per unit will be raised to $96.00, effective January 1, 1996, in order to keep up with escalating insurance, utility fees, and maintenance costs.

Remember, the dues must be paid on or before the first of each month. There is a $10.00 late fee after the 20th. If you have questions regarding your account or your payment history, feel free to call Cindy Anderson, bookkeeper for Sierra Loma Association.

BOARD MEETING DATES
The Board of Directors' meetings are held on the third Wednesday of each month at the Clubhouse, starting at 7:00 p.m. All owners are welcome to attend.

There are four basic steps to creating this document: (1) creating the heading (or title); (2) entering text; (3) specifying the column format; and (4) adding graphics.

Any graphics figures can be inserted either as you enter text or after all text has been entered. You will be saving your document using different file-names at various stages of creation. This way, should you make a mistake with your document, you can start from the previous step.

Depending on the font and character size you use, your document may not look the same as shown in this manual. The example in this manual uses various sizes of Times New Roman.

CREATING THE HEADING (TITLE)

You will first insert the text for title. As you noticed, the title for the news-letter is in characters larger than normal. The character size can be changed by using different sizes as discussed in Lesson 2. You will use 24-point characters.

- Click on the arrow next to the size indicator on the Formatting toolbar or from the Format menu, then select Font to change the point size to 24.

- Type **SIERRA LOMA LOG** centered on the line.

P R A C T I C E   T I M E   4 - 1

1. Enter the second line of the title, **Newsletter for Sierra Loma Homeowners Association**. The text is to be centered and entered using 12 point type.

2. Insert a blank line (press ⸤Enter⸥ twice).

3. Enter the date **October, 1995** right-justified in 10 point type.

4. Press ⸤Enter⸥. (Make sure that there is one blank line between the date and the end mark.)

5. Make the entire heading bold.

6. Save the document as **WD4A** on your data disk.

Your document should look like the one shown in Figure 4-2.

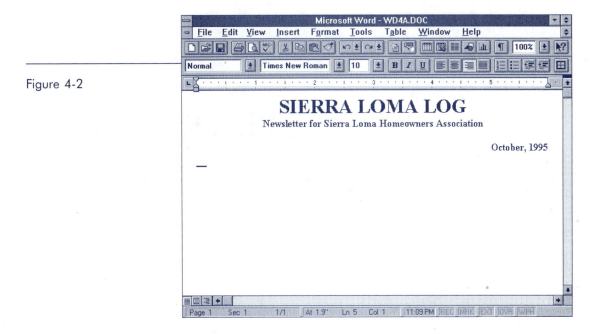

Figure 4-2

INSERTING A HORIZONTAL LINE

You will use the Border command in the Format menu to insert the line. Although a border can be inserted from the Format menu's Borders and Shading command, you will use the tool button here.

■   You may want to show all non-printing characters so that you know exactly where you are positioning the insertion point. Remember, this is done from the Tools menu's Option command.

■   Position the insertion point to the right of the date, and drag upward to select the entire text.

■   Click on the Border tool button, at the mouse pointer in Figure 4-3.

▶   *The Border toolbar is inserted, as shown in Figure 4-3.*

Various buttons on the toolbar let you insert a line above the selection, below the selection, at the left edge, right edge, and so on. Also, the leftmost selection lets you specify the thickness of the line.

■   Click on the down arrow at the right of the line width selector, then select 2¼ point as the width.

■   Specify drawing line at the bottom of the selected text. That is, click on the second button from the left.

▶   *The line has been inserted.*

■   Save the document as **WD4B** on your data disk.

Figure 4-3

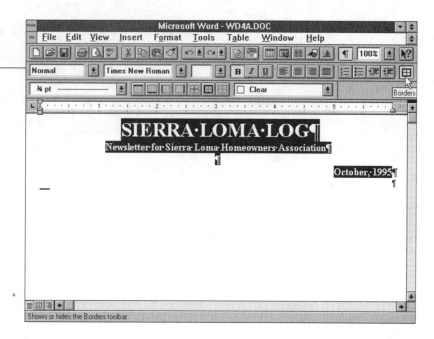

- Click on the Border tool button again to return to the normal mode.

- Position the insertion point on the blank line below the border.

You will now insert the text for the newsletter. The text will be long enough to cover two columns.

- Press [Enter] to insert a blank line.

- Change the alignment to Left.

- Enter the following text in 12-point type. The headings are in bold.

HOSE BIBS
Many residents have not disconnected their hoses from the outside hose bib since we have had such warm weather. The hose will act as a vacuum and trap the water inside the faucet extension behind the wall. When the water freezes and expands, the pipe may crack under the pressure of the ice. Then when the hose is used, the water runs under your house or into the wall causing substantial damage. Please disconnect your hoses. Should you have a problem, the Association will not be responsible for either the repair to the hose bib or the resulting damage to your home.

HEAT IN UNOCCUPIED UNITS
If your unit is left vacant, it is important to leave enough heat so as to prevent your water pipes from freezing. Any subsequent damage resulting from frozen pipes will be the homeowner's responsibility, and not subject to insurance claims.

WINDOW WASHING
The Association has had several inquiries as to homeowners wanting their windows washed. The Association does not provide this service. If you check the Yellow Pages, there are several licensed and insured companies available.

MAINTENANCE AND LANDSCAPE
There will be a "skeleton" maintenance crew from November 1, 1995, through March, 1996. Should, if, or when we have snow, they will be shoveling it from the walks. For your safety, please do not use salt of any kind on the sidewalks. The snow melts when the salt is applied, and refreezes to a slick, icy and dangerous condition. If you have an area needing "special attention," contact Fred Leisler, maintenance supervisor, at 747-7600.

ASSOCIATION DUES
The monthly homeowners dues per unit will be raised to $96.00, effective January 1, 1996, in order to keep up with escalating insurance, utility fees, and maintenance costs.

Remember, the dues must be paid on or before the first of each month. There is a $10.00 late fee after the 20th. If you have questions regarding your account or your payment history, feel free to call Cindy Anderson, bookkeeper for Sierra Loma Association.

BOARD MEETING DATES
The Board of Directors' meetings are held on the third Wednesday of each month at the Clubhouse, starting at 7:00 p.m. All owners are welcome to attend.

- Check spelling, then save as **WD4C**.

CREATING NEWSPAPER-TYPE COLUMNS

Now you are ready to define the columns, but first let's change the view so that the true layout of the document is displayed onscreen.

- From the View menu, select Page Layout.

    ▶ *The display shows the true layout of the document.*

- Place the insertion point before the word "Hose" on the first line of text.

- Click on the Column button 🔳 on the toolbar. You will see a small diagram that represents four columns, as shown in Figure 4-4.

Figure 4-4

■ Click on the second column from the left to indicate two columns.

▶ *The entire document appears in two columns, not just the*
text from the insertion point down. You can see the result
on the Print Preview screen shown in Figure 4-5.

Figure 4-5

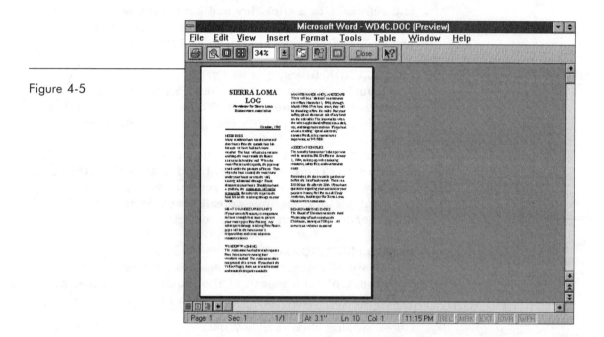

If you want some of the text on a page to cross multiple columns, the
page must be divided into two **sections**—one formatted to one column, and
the other to two columns. Ordinarily, you would create a section by inserting a section break at the appropriate location and defining display format
for each section. However, right now, you will use the Column command to
do both.

■ Click on the Column tool button, and select the first column in
the diagram to put the entire document back in one column.

■ Make sure that the insertion point is located just before the
word "Hose" on the first line of text.

■ From the Format menu, select Columns.

▶ *The Columns dialog box is displayed, as shown in*
Figure 4-6.

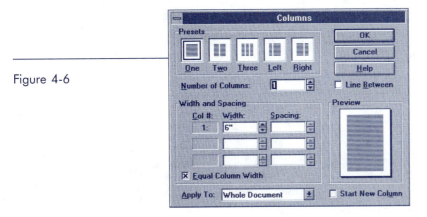

Figure 4-6

- Type **2** in the Number of Columns text box.
- Click on the down arrow key on the Apply To box.
- Select This Point Forward, then complete the command.

    ▶ *The document is in two columns from the insertion point down.*

- Save the file as **WD4D** on your data disk.

ADDING GRAPHIC PICTURES

You now decide that it might be nice to add a picture. You will insert the picture in the file houses.wmf at the beginning of the section "Heat in Unoccupied Units."

NOTE: If the standard installation procedure for Microsoft Word was followed, this picture is available in the Clipart directory within the directory containing Microsoft Word. You may want to check with your instructor to be sure.

- Place the insertion point at the beginning of the article on "Heat in Unoccupied Units." Be sure the insertion point is at the body of the article, not the heading.
- From the Insert menu, select Picture.

    ▶ *The Insert Picture dialog box, as shown in Figure 4-7, is displayed.*

- Specify the appropriate drive and directory where Microsoft Word clipart is found.
- Select the file houses.wmf in the Find Name list box.

    ▶ *The image appears in the Preview display.*

Figure 4-7

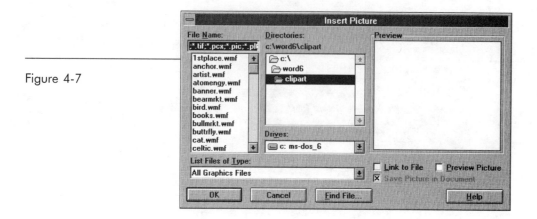

- ■ Complete the command.

  ▶ *The picture is inserted at the insertion point position, as shown in Figure 4-8.*

Figure 4-8

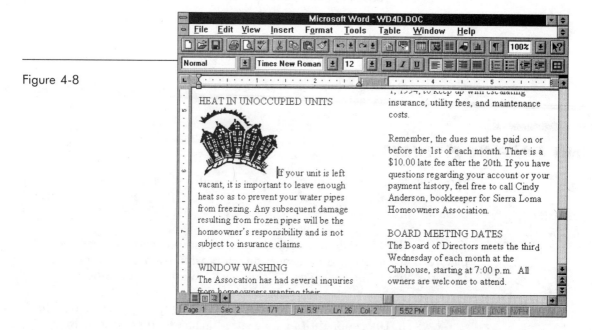

The picture is too big. You can change the size, however.

- ■ Click on the picture.

  ▶ *A box appears around the picture, as shown in Figure 4-9.*

The little black squares on the box are called ***handles***. These are used to change the size of the picture.

- ■ Position the mouse on the lower-right handle and drag the handle slightly up and to the left until the picture is about half the original size.

Figure 4-9

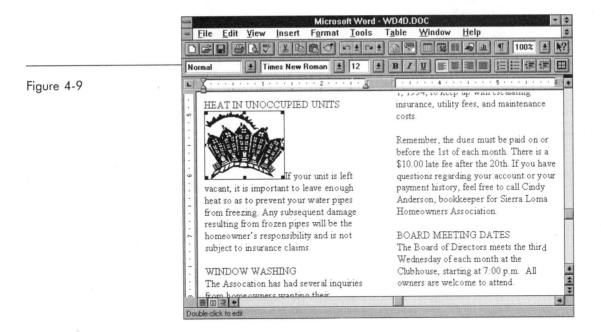

You might notice that the area to the right of the picture is left blank. That is, text is not wrapping around the picture. You can change this, too.

■   Make sure that the picture is still selected.

■   From the Insert menu, select Frame.

▶   *The text now wraps around the picture, as shown in Figure 4-10.*

Figure 4-10

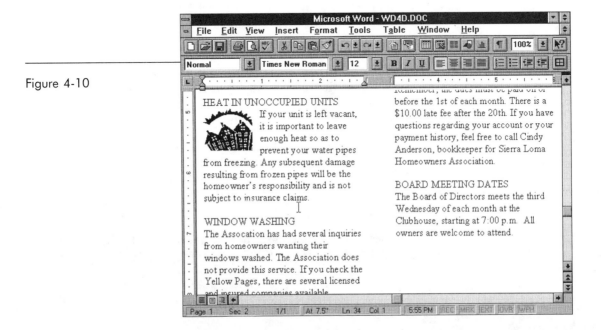

■   Save your file as **WD4E**.

■   Print the document.

USING TEMPLATES

A document ***template*** is a special document you can use as a pattern to create other documents of the same type. For example, you can use a letter template to produce letters that follow the same format. When you use a template, you needn't start from scratch each time you create a document. Tasks such as setting the margins, choosing a font, and creating headers and footers have already been done.

As explained earlier, every Word document is based on a template called Normal. That is, if you don't select a template when you create a new document, Word bases the new document on the Normal template. Any existing document can be made into a template by specifying it as a Document Template in the File Type.

You may wonder why you need a template. You can always open a document and edit it to suit your needs. However, when you do this, you have to make sure that you do not save the file using the same filename, thus destroying the original. When you open a template file, the new document will have the standard default name, such as Document 1.

Right now, you will create a memo using the memo2.dot template.

■   From the File menu, select New.

▶   *The New dialog box is displayed.*

■   Scroll the Template list box to select Memo2, then complete the command.

▶   *A new document opens, displaying the template, as shown in Figure 4-11.*

You can see that the memo has already been laid out nicely and the current date has already been entered. All you need to do is to substitute your entries to those enclosed in brackets.

■   Drag to select [*Names*] that follows "TO:."

■   Type **John Callahan**.

■   Drag to select [*Names*] that follows "FROM:."

■   Type ***your name***.

■   Similarly, enter **Cost Estimate** as the entry to follow "RE:" and type **Michael Myers** as the name to follow "CC:."

Figure 4-11

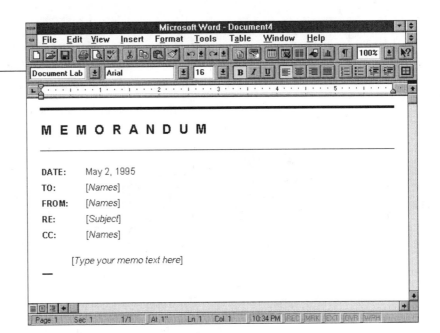

- For the text, drag to select [*Type your memo text here*], then type the following:

  As per our conversation, the following is a cost estimate for a new computer for your office.

- Press Enter twice to insert a blank line.

- Save the document as **MEMO1** on your data disk.

Next, you want to insert a table showing various costs.

INSERTING TABLES

Microsoft Word's ***table*** feature lets you add a grid to a document and fill it with text. This feature can be used to create a variety of documents, including forms, calendars, and documents similar to spreadsheets. Tables can perform simple arithmetic calculations, similar to the calculations a spreadsheet program can perform.

Before you begin working with tables, you must learn the basic vocabulary associated with them. Tables are made up of ***rows***, which run horizontally across the page, and ***columns***, which run vertically down the page. Rows are assigned numbers (starting with number 1 and going down the page), and columns are assigned letters of the alphabet (starting with A). The location where a row and column intersect is called a ***cell***. Cells are assigned names based on their relative position within the table. The cell at column C, row 4 is referred to as cell C4.

Using tables is a two-step process. First, you create the table by defining the number of columns and rows that make up the table. The second step is adding the text and numbers to the table.

■   From the T̲ables menu, select I̲nsert Table.

▶   *The Create Tables dialog box is displayed as shown in Figure 4-12.*

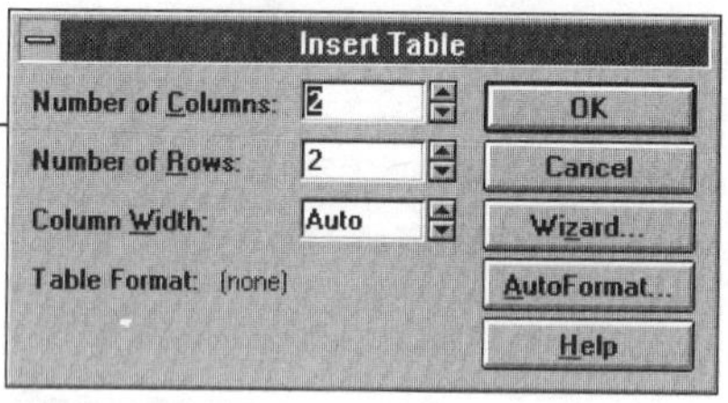

Figure 4-12

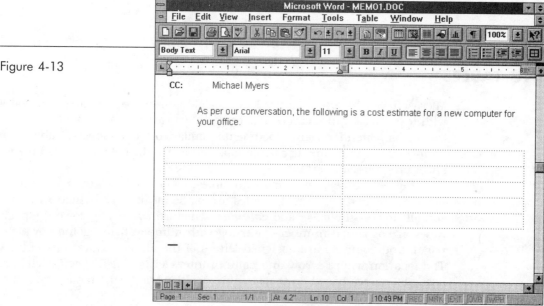

You need to enter the number of columns and rows to be created for the table. Here, you want two columns and five rows.

■   Enter **2** for the number of columns and **5** for the number of rows.

■   Complete the command.

Alternative: You can also specify the number of rows and columns through the Column button ▦ by dragging the mouse to the appropriate row and column on the grid that is displayed.

▶   *A table with the appropriate number of rows and columns is inserted, as shown in Figure 4-13. The insertion point is located in cell A1.*

Figure 4-13

■ Type the following information in cell A1. The text will wrap within the cell, so there is no need for you to press [Enter] at the edge of the cell.

486DX with 8 MB RAM, dual floppy, 120 MB Hard Disk, extended keyboard

■ Position the insertion point in cell B1 by pressing [Tab] or clicking in the cell.

■ Type **1299**.

■ Enter the following in the cells indicated:

cell A2   **Super VGA monitor**

cell B2   **350**

cell A3   **Mouse, DOS, Windows**

cell B3   **85**

cell A4   **Ethernet Card**

cell B4   **69**

cell A5   **TOTAL**

You look at the screen and decide that the first column should be wider.

■ Position the mouse pointer on the line between two columns.

▶ *The pointer changes, as shown in Figure 4-14.*

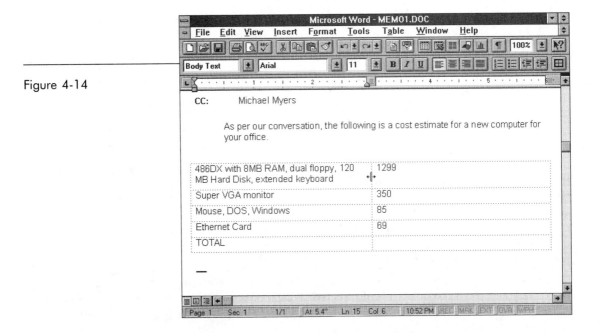

Figure 4-14

■ Drag the line to the right, to the 4″ position on the ruler. That is, hold down the left mouse button and move the mouse pointer to the right. When you are at the 4″ position, release the mouse button.

▶ *The column width, as well as the text in cells, adjust.*

PRACTICE TIME 4-2

Drag the left edge of the table to the right so that it is aligned to the paragraph above.

Figure 4-15 shows the correct alignment.

Figure 4-15

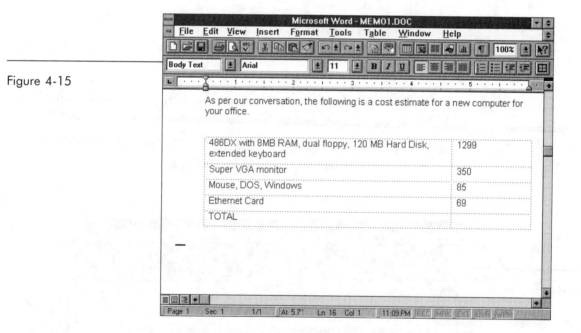

Since the second column contains monetary figures, you'd like to change the way it is displayed. First you need to select the column.

■ Position the insertion point in cell B1.

■ From the Table menu, select Select Column.

▶ *The column is selected.*

The following are two alternatives for selecting a column.

To select a column using the *keyboard*, position the insertion point in cell B1, then hold down the Shift key and press the ↓ key repeatedly.

To select a column using the *mouse*, move the mouse pointer just above the top border of cell B1 so that the mouse pointer turns into an arrow, as shown in Figure 4-16, then click the left button on the mouse.

Figure 4-16

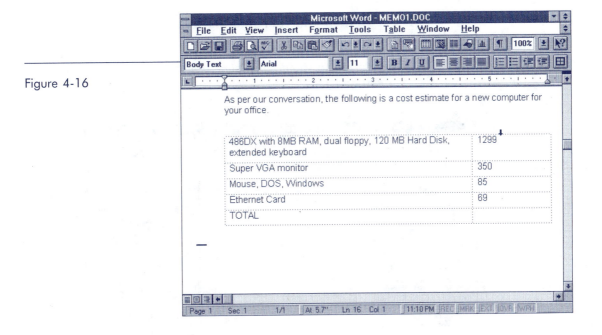

Now you can change the display format of column B.

■   Change the alignment to Right using either the Format, Paragraph command or the tool button.

In cell B5, you want to display the total cost.

■   Position the insertion point in cell B5.

■   From the Table menu, select Formula.

▶   *The Formula dialog box appears as shown in Figure 4-17.*

Notice that the default formula is the one to sum the entries above.

Figure 4-17

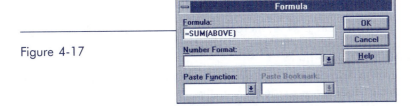

■   Complete the command.

▶   *The sum of values in cells B1 through B4 appears in cell B5.*

■   Position the insertion point below the table.

■   Insert a blank line.

■   Finish the memo by entering the text below:

If I can provide further information, please feel free to call me.

▶   *Your memo should look similar to the one displayed in Figure 4-18.*

Figure 4-18

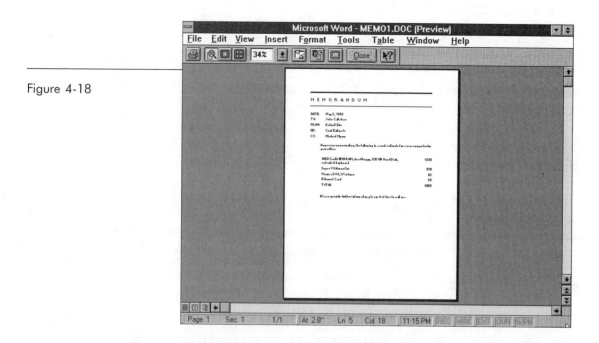

■   Save the document as file **MEMO2** on your data disk.

ENDING LESSON 4

There are many more features to Microsoft Word; these should be explored on your own. Just remember, the only way to learn to use a word processor is by working on the computer.

Exit Microsoft Word and Windows as explained in Lesson 1. There is no need to save changes you made to your file.

SUMMARY

- ☐ **The four basic steps in creating newspaper-type documents are: (1) Creating the title; (2) Entering text; (3) Defining the format; and (4) adding graphics.**

- ☐ **A line can be inserted in a document using the Border command in the Format menu.**

- ☐ **A graphic picture can be inserted in a document as text is being entered or after all text has been entered.**

- ☐ **A graphic picture can be sized using the handles.**

- ☐ **A document template is a special file you can use as a pattern to create other documents of the same type.**

- ☐ **The table feature lets you add a grid to a document and fill it with text. It can even perform some simple calculations similar to the ones used in spreadsheet programs.**

KEY TERMS

cell	rows	table
column	section	template
handles		

COMMAND SUMMARY

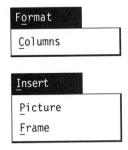

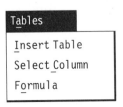

REVIEW QUESTIONS

1. Explain the steps involved in inserting a horizontal line using the Border command.

2. When using the Column tool button to specify the number of columns, how do you indicate two columns?

3. What do you have to do to display both single-column text and double-column text on a single page?

4. When you insert a graphic picture, where is it inserted within a document?

5. How do you change the size of a graphic picture?

6. What command do you give to make text wrap around a graphic picture?

7. What is a template?

8. Define the following terms: row, columns, and cell.

9. How do you change the column width of a table?

10. How do you display total of all values that appear above a given cell?

EXERCISES

1. Create a résumé using a template.
   a. Save it as **WD4EX1** on your data disk.
   b. Print the résumé.

2. Create the document shown in Figure 4-19. The graphics picture is disk.wmf in the Clipart directory of the MS Word directory.
   a. Save the document as **WD4EX2**.
   b. Print the document.

Figure 4-19

Care and Handling of Floppy Disks

 You must use proper care in handling floppy disks. They are very fragile. Here are some suggestions for their care and handling:

Insert the disk in disk drive, access window (for 5 1/4") or disk drive metal (for 3 1/2") end first, label side up.

- For 5 1/4" disk, always keep the disk in its envelope when not in use.
- For 3 1/2" disk, never open the mechanical shutter while a disk is out of the drive. Doing this exposes the surface to dirt, dust, fingerprints, etc.
- Do not touch the surface of the disk through the access window or wipe the surface with rags or tissue paper.
- Do not let disks collect dust.
- Keep disks out of the sun and away from other sources of heat, which can cause them to warp or lose data.
- Keep disks at least 2 feet away from magnetic fields, such as those generated by electrical motors, radios, televisions, tape recorders, library theft detectors, and other devices. A strong magnetic field will erase information on a disk.
- When writing on a disk label already attached to the disk, use only a felt-tipped pen. Never use any sort of instrument with a sharp point. Also, never use an eraser. Eraser dust is abrasive and may get on the mylar surface.
- Keep disks at room temperature before use (a disk just brought in from a cold blizzard has shrunk enough in size that its tracks are not where the system expects to find them).
- Never open the drive door or remove a disk while the drive is running--that is, while the red in-use light on the front of the disk drive is on. If you do, you can damage the data on your disk.
- Check to make sure that the gummed tab and external labels are on securely.

3. Create the document shown in Figure 4-20. The graphics picture is computer.wmf in the Clipart directory of the MS Word directory.

   a. Save the document as **WD4EX3**.

   b. Print the newsletter.

Figure 4-20

CAMPUS COMPUTER CLUB
WEEKLY NEWSLETTER

Volume 5, No. 2   October 7, 1993

SEMESTER DUES DUE
Fall semester dues of $5.00, to help cover the cost of computer paper and online file storage, are due by October 10. A fee of $10.00 will be assessed to those who are late with dues.

FALL WORKSHOP SCHEDULE
Due to a mix-up in scheduling with the Computer Science Department's seminars, the Campus Computer Club seminars schedule published last week is void. Please stay tuned for a revised schedule.

IMPORTANT ANNOUNCEMENT
Anyone attempting to infect the campus computer with a worm or virus will be prosecuted. See next item for related info.

SEMINAR SPEAKER
FBI agent Mort Merriweather will speak next Friday at 3 p.m. on Computer Bugs, Worms, and Viruses. Mort has been involved in several Federal investigations of computer chaos. He says he will give some hints on keeping personal computers "well," and will show us some examples of destructive viruses (including the penalties that their perpetrators incurred).

THIS WEEK'S TIP
Keep your files in order. Use the TIDY_FILE utility written by Kitty Hawkins to delete obsolete versions that clutter disk space. See Chet Williams in the Lab for details.

TWENTY YEARS AGO
Randy Kondo's father has provided us with a newsletter that the computer club published in 1969. An enlarged photocopy is available in our office for those of you interested in stone age computing. To wit:

The IBM 1620 in use has a memory size of 20,000 characters.

Users can submit one job per day on punched cards.

The new card reader reads 10 cards per second.

The newsletter doesn't say it, but there is no on-line storage for student programs or data, and no magnetic tape drives.

The programming languages most used are FORTRAN IV and Assembler.

The newsletter is typed, get this, using a manual typewriter!

Word 6.0 Projects

PROJECT 1

1. Create the memo shown below, save it as **WDP1**, and print it.

   MEMORANDUM

   DATE: *current date*

   TO: **Dallas Irving, President**

   FROM: *your name*

   SUBJECT: **Water Saddle Market Evaluation**

   Our recent survey of market prospects for the water saddle yielded the following conclusions.

   1. **The projected sales for five years should be about 1,600 saddles.**

   2. **The dude ranch market is but one of three viable markets: private owners and horseback riding stables are other strong markets.**

   3. **It is important to get in first with a quality product. Potential buyers are very conservative. If our initial product has serious flaws, all our subsequent products will not sell.**

   4. **Cowpokes, Inc. is currently well-positioned to enter this market.**

   Some details of our findings include the following items.

   Breakdown by Market and Year

Year	Dude Ranches	Privates	Horse Rides	Total
1	50	100	50	200
2	100	100	50	250
3	150	100	50	300
4	200	100	100	400
5	250	100	100	450
Total	750	500	350	1600

<u>**Consumer Concerns about a New Product**</u>

- **Is it produced by a company that can be relied upon?**
- **Does it represent an improvement, not just a trendy twist?**
- **Is it reasonably priced?**
- **Is it durable?**

PROJECT 2

1. Enter the following in the data source file to be used in a merge. Save it as file **WDP2DAT** on your data disk.

Field Definition

Field 1	**Borrower**
Field 2	**Lender**
Field 3	**Principal**
Field 4	**Payment**
Field 5	**Date**
Field 6	**Rate**
Field 7	**City**
Field 8	**State**
Field 9	**Day**
Field 10	**Month**
Field 11	**Year**

Data to Be Entered

Field 1	**Marty Python**	Field 1	**Roni Andrews**
Field 2	**Bank of Arizona**	Field 2	**Bank of Nevada**
Field 3	**$100,000**	Field 3	**$67,000**
Field 4	**$1,300**	Field 4	**$612.88**
Field 5	**May 11, 1995**	Field 5	**October 14, 1995**
Field 6	**10%**	Field 6	**10.5%**
Field 7	**Phoenix**	Field 7	**Reno**
Field 8	**Arizona**	Field 8	**Nevada**
Field 9	**11**	Field 9	**14**

Field 10 **November**   Field 10 **September**

Field 11 **1994**   Field 11 **1994**

2. Enter the following document as the main document to be used in a merge. Save it as **WDPMAIN** on your data disk.

Promissory Note

The <BORROWER> agrees to pay <LENDER> the principal sum of <PRINCIPAL>. By this note, <BORROWER> agrees to make monthly installments in the sum of <PAYMENT> or more, until said obligation is paid in full. The first payment is due on or before <DATE>, and all successive payments are due on the first day of each succeeding month thereafter until paid in full.

This obligation shall bear interest on the declining principal balance at a rate of <RATE> per annum. In the event the undersigned fails to make a required payment within thirty days when due, then the remaining balance of the obligation shall become due and payable in full. Furthermore, if <BORROWER> is more than 30 days late on a required payment, <LENDER> can elect to recover the collateral securing this obligation, as described below, and dispose of same in any commercially reasonable manner, applying the proceeds of such sale toward the balance remaining hereon.

Additional payments or prepayment in full may be paid by <BORROWER> without penalty.

No delay on the part of <LENDER> in the exercise of any right or remedy shall operate as a waiver thereof, and no single partial exercise by the same of any right or remedy shall preclude further exercise of any right or remedy.

The obligation evidenced hereby has been made in <CITY,> <STATE>, and shall be governed by the laws of the State of <STATE>.

Dated this <DAY> day of <MONTH>, <YEAR>.

_____

<BORROWER>, borrower

_____

<LENDER>, lender

3. Merge the files and get a printout.

Microsoft Word 6.0 for Windows Command Summary

This section is a quick reference for Microsoft Word commands covered in this manual. This is *not* a complete list of all Microsoft Word commands.

Command	from Menu	Shortcut
Alignment	Format, Paragraph	
Center text		Ctrl+E or ▦
Justified		Ctrl+J or ▦
Left alignment		Ctrl+L or ▦
Right alignment		Ctrl+R or ▦
Appearance	Format, Font	
Bold		Ctrl+B or **B**
Italic		Ctrl+I or *I*
Underline		Ctrl+U or U
Arranging window	Window, Arrange All	
Bullet		▦
Column	Format, Columns	▦
Copy a text	Edit, Copy	Ctrl+C or ▦
Cut a text	Edit, Cut	Ctrl+X or ▦
Date—inserting current	Insert, Date and Time	
Display actual layout	View, Page Layout	
Display non-printing characters	Tools, Options	¶
Display ruler	View, Ruler	
Exit Word	File, Exit	Alt+F4
Find text	Edit, Find	Ctrl+F
Font	Format, Font	formatting toolbar
Frame—insert	Insert, Frame	
Header or footer	View, Header and Footer	
Help	Help, Contents	F1 ▦

Command	from Menu	Shortcut
Insert a horizontal line	Format, Borders and Shading	⊞
Line indentation	Format, Paragraph	ruler
Line spacing	Format, Paragraph	
Margin Setting	File, Page Setup, Margins	ruler
Merge document	Tools, Mail Merge	
Open an existing document	File, Open	Ctrl+O or 🖿
Open a new document	File, New	Ctrl+N or 🗋
Page break	Insert, Break	Ctrl+Enter
Page numbering	Insert, Page Numbers	
Paper orientation	File, Page Setup, Paper Size	
Paragraph indentation	Format, Paragraph	🔲 or ruler
Paste text	Edit, Paste	Ctrl+V or 🖹
Pictures—insert	Insert, Picture	
Preview a file	File, Preview	🔍
Print a file	File, Print	Ctrl+P or 🖨
Replace text	Edit, Replace	Ctrl+H
Save file with new name	File, Save As	
Save file with same name	File, Save	Ctrl+S or 🖫
Size of characters	Format, Font	formatting toolbar
Spelling check	Tools, Spelling …	✓
Tables		
Insert a table	Tables, Insert Table	▦
Select a column	Tables, Select Column	
Insert a formula	Tables, Formula	
Tabs	Format, Tabs	ruler
Thesaurus	Tools, Thesaurus	Shift+F7
Undo typing	Edit, Undo Typing	Ctrl+Z or ↺
Windows—switching	Window, filename	

Glossary

active window The window to which the next command will apply. If a window is active, its title bar changes color to differentiate it from other windows.

align To line up.

application window A window that contains a running application. The name of the application appears at the top of this window.

border The outer edge of a window.

bullets A text format in which each item in a list of items is preceded by a small circle.

byte A single character.

cell Intersection of a row and a column in a table.

centered Text that is centered, line by line, on the page.

check box A small square box that appears in a dialog box and that can be selected or cleared. When the check box is selected, an X appears in the window.

click To press and release a mouse button quickly.

clipboard The temporary storage location used to transfer data between documents and between applications.

close To remove a document window or application window from the desktop.

collapse a directory To hide additional directory levels below a selected directory.

configuration The arrangement of hardware and software in a computer system.

control menu box The icon that opens the control menu for the window. It is always at the left of the title bar.

column Vertical entries in a table.

cpi (characters per inch) A measurement of type size.

current directory The directory that is currently highlighted in the directory tree or whose directory window is the active window.

cursor A symbol or flashing underscore that shows the position onscreen where an entry is made.

cut To remove selected text from a document and place it temporarily on the clipboard; the text can then be pasted to a new location.

data source In a merge operation, the file that contains the data to be merged into the main document.

default A value, action, or setting that is automatically used when no alternate instructions are given. For example, the default drive is where the program looks for data files unless explicitly instructed otherwise.

desktop The screen background for Windows on which windows, icons, and dialog boxes appear.

dialog box A rectangular box that either requests or provides information. Many dialog boxes present options to choose among before Windows can carry out a command. Some dialog boxes present warnings or explain why a command cannot be completed.

dictionary A list of correctly spelled words used by the Speller.

directory A file or a part of a disk that contains the names and locations of other files on the disk.

directory tree A graphic display in File Manager of the directory structure of a disk.

document window A window within an application window that contains a document you create or modify by using an application. There can be more than one document window in an application window.

double-click To rapidly press and release a mouse button twice without moving the mouse. Double-clicking usually carries out an action, such as opening an icon.

drag   To hold down the mouse button while moving the mouse.

drag and drop   To move an item onscreen by pointing to it, then dragging it to the desired position.

drop-down list box   A single-line dialog box that opens to display a list of choices.

drop-down menu   The sub-option menu that appears when an option in the menu bar is highlighted.

endmark   An underscore that shows the end of the document.

expand directory   To show currently hidden levels in the directory tree.

field   A distinct data element used in the merge feature. Each record in a secondary file is composed of fields.

file   A collection of data records with related content; data stored as a named unit on a peripheral storage medium such as a disk.

filename   The name assigned a file; must be no more than eight characters long, and may include an optional extension of a period plus up to three characters.

find   A utility that allows you to look for all occurrences of specific words or characters in a document.

first-line indent marker   A symbol on the ruler that indicates how far the first line of paragraph is to be indented.

font   The appearance of characters on your screen and printout, which is determined by the typeface, size, and special treatment such as bold, underline, italics, and so on.

footer   Lines of text that appear at the bottom of every page.

frame   A container into which you can put an object (such as a graphic). Once an object is in a frame, it can be dragged to anywhere in the page.

format a disk   To prepare a blank disk to receive data.

function keys   Keys ($\boxed{F1}$ to $\boxed{F10}$ or $\boxed{F12}$) that allow special functions to be entered with a single keystroke.

group   A collection of programs in Program Manager. Grouping your programs makes them easier to find when you want to start them.

group icon   The graphic that represents a minimized Program Manager group. Double-clicking on the group icon opens the group window.

group window   A window that displays the items in a group within Program Manager.

handles   Black squares that appear on the box around a graphic that can be used to change the size of the picture.

hanging indent   Text layout in which the first line of a paragraph is flush left, while runover lines are indented.

hard page break   A page break code that is specially inserted into the text.

header   Lines of text that appear at the top of every page.

header record   In a merge, the first row of the data source where field names appear. The header records act as column headings for the information on the data source.

I-beam   The shape taken by the mouse pointer when it is in the workspace.

icon   A graphic representation of various elements in Windows, such as disk drives, files, applications, and documents.

inactive window   Any open window in which you are not currently working.

insert mode   An editing mode in which the characters you type are inserted at the insertion point, pushing previous characters tothe right.

insertion point   The place where text will be inserted when you next type a character.

justified   Text that is aligned on both the left and right margins.

landscape   Paper orientation in which the document is wider than it is long.

launching   Starting an application program. This is usually done by double-clicking on the application icon.

left-aligned   Text that is aligned on the left margin.

left indent marker   A symbol on the ruler that shows how far the text is to be indented from the left margin.

list box   Within a dialog box, a box listing available choices, for example, the list of all available files in a directory. If all the choices won't fit, the list box has a vertical scroll bar.

main document   The file containing the document in a merge operation. Using the merge feature, you can print multiple copies, each incorporating data in the data file.

maximize button   The small box containing an up arrow at the right of the title bar. It can be clicked to enlarge a window to its maximum size.

menu   A list of items, most of which are commands. Menu names appear in the menu bar near the top of the window.

menu bar   The horizontal bar containing the menu choices.

merge   A feature that allows you to insert the data from a data source into specified positions in the main document.

minimize button   The small box containing a down arrow at the right of the title bar. It can be clicked to shrink a window to an icon.

monospaced characters   A font in which all letters have the same width.

mouse   A cursor-control device that resembles a small box on wheels. As the box is rolled on a flat surface, the movement of the wheel signals the computer to move the cursor on the display screen in direct proportion to the movement of the mouse.

multitasking   The ability to run more than one application at a time without interrupting the execution of any of the active applications.

newspaper-style columns   Text format in which there are multiple columns on a single page. Text flows from column to column.

non-printing characters   Special characters entered into a document to indicate where certain keys, such as [Enter] and [Tab], were pressed. These characters are not displayed when the document is printed.

open   To display the contents of a file in a window or to enlarge an icon to a window.

page layout view   Document display which reflects the way document will be printed.

paste   To insert text from the clipboard to a new location in a document; see cut.

pathname   The direction to a directory or file within your system. For example, C:\DIR1\FILEA is the pathname for the FILEA file in the DIR1 subdirectory on drive C.

point   To move the pointer onscreen until it rests on the item you want to select.

point size   The unit of measure commonly used to indicate font size. There are 72 points to an inch.

pointer   The arrow-shaped cursor on the screen that indicates the position of the mouse.

portrait   Paper orientation in which a sheet is longer than it is wide.

print preview   The feature that allows you to view the text onscreen as it will be printed.

program group   See group.

proportionally spaced characters   Font that uses varying widths for different letters; for example, an *m* is wider than an *i*, as it is here.

record   A single block of data used in the merge feature. Each block of data pertaining to a separate person or item is a record.

replace   A utility that searches for all occurrences of specific words or characters and replaces them with words or characters you specify.

restore button   The small box at the right of the title bar that contains a down arrow and an up arrow. The restore button appears after you have enlarged a window to its full size. It can be clicked to return the window to its previous size.

right-aligned   Text that is aligned on the right margin.

right indent marker   A symbol on the ruler that shows how far the text is to be indented from the right margin.

row   Horizontal entries in a table.

ruler   The bar at the top of the workspace that displays current settings for margins, tabs, justification, and spacing.

scroll   To move through a document by moving lines off the top or bottom of the screen. Word does this automatically as you enter text, or you can scroll through a document using the scroll bar.

section   A portion of the text. A section can be as short as a single paragraph or as long as an entire document. Each section can be formatted differently.

selection bar   An unmarked area along the left side of the text area. It is used to select text with the mouse. When the mouse pointer is in the selection bar, it turns into a right-pointing arrow.

soft font   A font that is downloaded to your printer's memory from a disk provided by the font's manufacturer.

soft page break   A page break that is inserted automatically by the program, based on specified margin and page length settings.

soft return   A line break that is inserted automatically by the program, based on specified margin settings.

status bar   A horizontal bar at the bottom of the document window that displays such information as the font style and type size being used and the insertion point position.

subdirectory   A directory contained within another directory. All directories are subdirectories of the root directory.

table   A grid that can be filled with text and numbers.

tabs   Settings that determine indents, or the new position of the insertion point each time you press Tab; by default, tabs are set at every half-inch.

task   An open application.

template   A special document you can use as a pattern to create other documents of the same type.

text area   The area of a window between the menu bar and the status bar which displays the document you are working with or information about the application you are working on.

text box   A box within a dialog box where you type information needed to carry out the chosen command.

title bar   The horizontal bar located at the top of a window containing the title of the window.

toggle   A command that alternatively turns a feature on and off.

tool bar   A section of the window containing buttons with icons, called tools, which you can click to perform certain operations.

typeface   The graphic style applied to characters; common typefaces are Courier, Helvetica, and Times Roman. The typeface is often referred to as the font.

typeover (OVR) mode   An editing mode that replaces the character the insertion point is on with the character you type.

window   A rectangular area onscreen in which you view an application or document.

wordwrap   A feature that automatically moves a word at the end of a line to the next line.

work area   The area of a window that displays the information contained in the application window of the document with which you are working.

zoom   A feature that allows you to look at the text preview screen close up or from a distance.

Index